NEW
MOVES

THE DREAMSEEKER MEMOIR SERIES

On an occasional and highly selective basis, books in the DreamSeeker Memoir Series, intended to make available fine memoirs by writers whose works at least implicitly arise from or engage Anabaptist-related contexts, themes, or interests, are published by Cascadia Publishing House LLC under the DreamSeeker Books imprint. Cascadia oversees content of these novels or story collections in collaboration with DreamSeeker Memoir Series Editor Jeff Gundy.

NEW MOVES

A Theological Odyssey

a memoir by

J. Denny Weaver

DreamSeeker Memoir Series, Volume 3

DreamSeeker Books
TELFORD, PENNSYLVANIA

an imprint of
Cascadia Publishing House LLC

Cascadia Publishing House orders, information, reprint permissions:
contact@CascadiaPublishingHouse.com
1-215-723-9125
126 Klingerman Road, Telford PA 18969
www.CascadiaPublishingHouse.com

Book design by Cascadia Publishing House
Cover design by Gwen M. Stamm

Bible quotations are used by permission, all rights reserved and, unless otherwise noted, are from *The New Revised Standard Version of the Bible*, copyright 1989, by the Division of Christian Education of the National Council of the Churches of Christ in the USA.

Library of Congress Cataloging-in-Publication Data

Names: Weaver, J. Denny, 1941- author.
Title: New moves : a theological odyssey : a memoir / by J. Denny
Weaver.
Description: Telford, Pennsylvania : DreamSeeker Books, an imprint of
Cascadia Publishing House LLC, [2023] | Series: DreamSeeker memoir
series ; 3 | Includes bibliographical references and index. | Summary:
"In his theological memoir, J. Denny Weaver tells how his career as a
theologian developed and led to his shaping a nonviolent understanding
of Jesus' Atonement"-- Provided by publisher.
Identifiers: LCCN 2023022814 | ISBN 9781680270242 (trade paper-
back)
Subjects: LCSH: Weaver, J. Denny, 1941- | Religious educators--United
States--Biography. | Nonviolence--Religious aspects--Christianity. |
Anabaptists--United States--Biography.
Classification: LCC BL43.W43 A3 2023 | DDC 289.7092 [B]--
dc23/eng20230913
LC record available at https://lccn.loc.gov/2023022814

29 28 27 26 25 24 23   10 9 8 7 6 5 4 3 2 1

For
Alvin and Velma,
who launched me on this odyssey
and
Mary,
who lived it

Contents

Castle

THREE: MIDDLE GAME

FOUR: END GAME

Storing the Pieces

Preface

Since the earliest anecdote in this story of my theological odyssey occurred when I was six, in one sense it feels like I have been working on it for my entire life. At another level, in 2008 I began jotting ideas down on scraps of paper and slipping these notes into a folder. Thus 2008 might serve as a starting point.

In 2018, my wife and I moved into an independent living apartment in Oakwood Village. That fall at Oakwood, I helped to start a writers group, which meets twice a month to share stories and poems. The first versions of some stories in this memoir came into being as accounts that I presented to the writers group.

Since real writing was involved, fall of 2018 might count as a start date for this memoir. Finally, in September of the unforgettable year of the pandemic of 2020, I did an online seminar on memoir writing. The eight items presented to that seminar appear in revised form in the account that follows. These items are the first that were written explicitly for this memoir. Thus 2020 might serve as a beginning point. Last, a recently formed writers group from Madison Mennonite Church has processed several vignettes and chapters with me. In any case, much of the formal writing occurred during the pandemic year of 2020, continued into 2021, and was completed in 2022 as the pandemic continued to percolate and a war has begun in Ukraine with no foreseeable end.

This work owes thanks to many people. They include the teachers that I have learned from, many of whom are no longer living. It includes the many students in my classes, who joined in my processing of issues and then asked questions that clarified understandings for them as well as for me. I owe much to the colleagues I have collaborated with and the colleagues I have argued with but whose challenges pushed me to develop my perspectives further. For those whose names appear in this book, know that I am grateful to all of you.

Meanwhile, thanks to the members of my Oakwood writers group for suggestions, corrections, support, and for laughing at what I intended to be humorous: Phil Hardacre, Nancy Kittleson, Alan Knox, Linda Meyer, Pat Meagher-Springer, Jack Naughton, George Peranteau, Dick Rossmiller, Sparrow Senty, Jim Taylor, Karen Waggoner.

In the seminar on memoir writing, I learned much about scene setting, description, and narrative arc, and received much encouragement. I am grateful to Instructor Christopher Chambers and to participants Peg Aaron, Scott Krizek, and Istiaq Mian. Members of the Madison Mennonite writers group who offered comments and valuable advice on specific chapters are Duane Beachey, Bonnie Berger-Durnbaugh, Evie Yoder Miller, David Serafy-Cox, and Bernie Wiebe. In addition, Coliér McNair and Gerald Mast read several sections and contributed valuable suggestions.

I am grateful to Jocelyn Milner, Mark Ediger, Valerie Showalter, Justin Shenk, Lorraine Stoltzfus, and Mary Weaver, who read the entire manuscript and offered a number of important suggestions that have strengthened the story. Lorraine, a proofreader *par excellence*, did double duty by also correcting the author corrections pages.

Finally, it is gratifying that publisher Michael A. King and series editor Jeff Gundy were willing to include this memoir in Cascadia's DreamSeeker Memoir Series. Michael supplied valuable advice on tone of the narrative, while Jeff raised a number of questions that I dealt with. Following their suggestions has made this a stronger book.

I made the chess set pictured on the cover. It is a copy of a set that an acquaintance brought from Poland, except that I adapted the design of knights and bishops. I began turning it on the lathe in my father's studio in Kansas City, Kansas, in 1986, and worked on it sporadically thereafter. I finally finished it in St. Louis in 2010 in the shop of my son-in-law Michael Kaufman. Kent Sweitzer, photographer *extraordinaire*, took the cover photo of a chess move, which serves as the book's metaphor for developing a new version of theology as well as the photos of pieces that grace the book's divider pages.

When the first edition of *The Nonviolent Atonement* was published, I sent a copy to my brother Gary, who was an internal medicine specialist. I accompanied the book with accounts of some of the incidents in the following pages. My brother in turn showed it to a colleague in his office. A couple weeks later, in the mail I received a small, carved wood giraffe. Gary explained that his colleague sends giraffes to people who stick out their necks. Since I had stuck out my neck to publish a book that challenged Anselm, she wanted me to have a giraffe. To this day that giraffe occupies a prominent place in our living room. Among other things, then, this memoir is an ode to a giraffe.

When my father died in 1993, I discovered three items of theology that he had preserved. One was a Mennonite Central Committee pamphlet on racism. A second was an MCC pamphlet on peace and nonviolence. The third was a small notebook, which held notes and outlines of a few presentations he had given at our church. One of these presentations was an outline of Harold S. Bender's "Anabaptist Vision." I have no memories of specific discussions of these issues with my father or mother, but it was a shock to find these items that represented three primary elements of my writing career. This memoir can stand as a memorial to my parents, Alvin and Velma Weaver, and what I did with their legacy to me.

Most of all I am grateful to my wife Mary. She has lived through the downs and ups of the story that follows and has encouraged what may be the last major contribution of my career as theologian.

—*J. Denny Weaver*
Madison, Wisconsin

Prologue

It was the fall of 2001, exact date forgotten. I was standing in my favorite classroom—the small, tiered amphitheater on the first floor of Centennial Hall at Bluffton College—and I was feeling good. The lectures had gone well with this class of twenty-five students. I had been particularly articulate in critiquing the received, presumed-standard, satisfaction image of atonement and posing my alternative. (For a summary of the received, standard image of atonement and my alternative, see the Theological Excursus at the end of the Introduction.) I asked if there were any questions. Answering student questions was my favorite classroom activity.

A student in the center of the top row raised her hand and asked, "What do you want to accomplish with your restructured view of atonement?" Names to argue with flitted through my mind, ever farther back in history, until I reached the source. After a few seconds reflection, with a grin, I answered, "I want to be known as the man who overturned Anselm."

I had been thinking about atonement for more than ten years, but this was the first time I had heard myself express the overthrow of Anselm aloud. It was a cheeky and audacious response, although no doubt the students lacked the perspective to know how far out the answer really was.

Anselm was the Archbishop of Canterbury, whose book *Why the God-Man*, published in 1099, has defined the presumed-standard, dominant, satisfaction image of atonement for at least the last 800 years. Professional theologians certainly

knew Anselm's name, but it would not have been known to the
many Christians who assume that any of the variants of his view
are simply the way salvation happens. For any of the variants,
the heart of the image is that God's salvation of sinners depends
on God receiving a blood sacrifice to pay the price for human sin.
Thus God the Father sent Jesus the Son to die for the sins of humankind.

Anselm's view is accepted as an unquestioned given by Fundamentalists, most Evangelicals, and many other Christians
who consider themselves orthodox. Thus when I said that I
wanted to be known as the man who overturned Anselm, I was
challenging a majority of the Christian tradition. It was as close
to an impossible, tilting-at-windmills goal as a junior theologian, unknown beyond the Mennonite theological guild, could
have. I was engaged in a project that was risky, stimulating, controversial, and at times exhilarating.

This book traces the path I followed to arrive at this audacious challenge, what happened when my book challenging
Anselm appeared a few months later, and what followed the appearance of the book—not all of which had to deal with Anselm.
Were any windmills damaged? Read on to find out.

Introduction

This theological memoir recounts the story of my effort to overturn Anselm, a pursuit that did attract some attention. One year at the annual meeting of the American Academy of Religion, I approached Wipf and Stock editor Robin Perry to inquire about interest in another manuscript I was developing. Perry eyed my name tag and asked, "Are you 'the atonement guy'?" I admitted that I was. One dimension of this book is a story of how I became "the atonement guy."

Developing a theology has some resemblance to playing chess. One is never done learning, and every move elicits a response, not all of which are anticipated, and those responses call forth other new moves. Like a chess match that develops one move at a time, theology is an ongoing conversation. Theology can reach a kind of conclusion, as with my books on atonement, but the conversation goes on, and the conclusions about atonement led to additional statements about God and nonviolence in unexpected places. Thus this memoir is about more than the pursuit of Anselm and continues on with the following stages of learning, well beyond atonement.

In the annals of chess, a match has distinct parts. One must set up the board, and then there are opening moves, the middle game, and the end game. The pieces go back in their box. As the Table of Contents of this memoir displays, I have thought about my career on that outline. Using this framework, there is the background and preparation I brought to my career as professor, the tentative early moves, the productive middle years, and a significant conclusion. I designated the interlude in Winnipeg at Canadian Mennonite Bible College as a Castle. Castle is a move in chess to put the king in a strong defensive position before the aggressive moves in the middle game. Here it signals a move between the end of my claim to be a Reformation scholar and the beginning of my career as a theologian, the identity I claimed for the remainder of my career.

No metaphor perfectly represents what it symbolizes. Although I described similarities between developing a theological position and learning to play chess, and I have organized the sections of this memoir according to the parts of a chess match, there are ways in which the metaphor falls short and even contradicts the nonviolent dimensions of my theology. Chess is inherently an individualist game between two sides, using pieces representing imperial hierarchy to force submission and defeat on the opponent—an implicitly violent result.

Admittedly, the account to follow does display an element of challenge and assertion of my view over others. However, rather than an individual activity, developing theology involves learning from teachers and colleagues, working within a church community, and collaborating with colleagues. Even disagreements contribute to better understanding. These dimensions are all visible in the story to follow.

A final weakness of the metaphor is that theology is not a mere game. It shapes the way that its adherents engage the world. My efforts at theology were about developing a way for the followers of Jesus to live his nonviolent life in the so-called real world.

It was a number of years before I realized where my career was heading, but now I can say that in a sense I have spent my career as a theology professor and theologian rethinking the entire theological enterprise, or rethinking how the church should do theology. This rethinking has produced opposition, some of it significant. Many theologians desire to stay with the received tradition. Reaction to my rethinking has ranged from "it's just your opinion" to "who are you to rethink the ancients" to comments of "thank you." The story to follow reflects versions of all these responses.

When in mid-career I decided to embrace my identity as a theologian, my intent was to produce theology that reflected a peace church orientation but was done in a way that included all Christians. By now I can say that this theology offered alternatives to parts of the standard, inherited theological tradition. My efforts dealt with Christology (how the church has talked about Jesus), atonement (the doctrine that discusses how Jesus saves), the nature of God, and the roles of violence or nonviolence in theology, along with a number of spin-offs. The following story provides an overview of my comprehensive theological outlook, and the positions that I have developed.

Of these issues, I gave the most attention to atonement theology, and the two editions of *The Nonviolent Atonement* became perhaps the most discussed part of my theological work. As preparation for the narrative to follow, the "Theological Excursus" at the end of this Introduction summarizes my critique of the received, satisfaction image and the nonviolent alternative that I proposed.

New Moves book is not an autobiography. It does not provide a chronology of my life nor mention all writing or every theological activity in which I engaged. It is a theological memoir, using selected stories and memories to tell the unfolding plot line of my career, from earliest theological memories to retirement and the conclusions I eventually reached. It is not always possible to know exactly when I first had an idea. Thus some things have been merged in the effort to provide a coherent narrative. Such a narrative may inevitably provide perspectives on events that differ from the accounts of other participants in those same events. In that case, the other participants are invited to write their own stories.

Along with my memories, the primary source for this memoir is the journal that I have kept on a near-daily basis since 1966. When there are references to events in the wider society, I have used external sources to verify dates, names of places, and facts related to events. Memories and the journal both have surprises. On some occasions, where I have a vivid memory of an event, the journal entry for that event is surprisingly sparse in its description. In other instances, the journal contains detailed accounts of events that had entirely escaped my memory. In the memoir, I have not tried to distinguish those two situations.

Theological Excursus

The theology of *The Nonviolent Atonement* constitutes the heart of my career-long theological contribution. Here is a thumbnail sketch of the book's argument. If readers so choose, they may skip the excursus and begin the narrative.

In the Gospels, as the embodiment of the reign of God on earth, Jesus confronted the powers of evil, represented by all the people and forces that opposed him and contributed to his death. They killed him, but God raised him, which was a victory for the reign of God over evil. Salvation comes through identifying with Jesus and participating in his victory in the reign of God. This image is a narrative *Christus Victor*, a narrative of the victorious Christ.

This story features a nonviolent God, in the sense that God did not kill Jesus nor send Jesus for the specific purpose of being killed. Rather than administering violence, in the face of violence, God restored life. God is the giver of life. Also note that unambiguously, the powers that killed Jesus oppose the reign of God and the will of God.

In the book of Revelation, the symbols display the church as the earthly representative of the reign of God as it confronts the powers of evil, represented by the Roman Empire. There are martyrs to the empire, but ultimately victory comes in the resurrection of Jesus. With the image of church confronting empire and victory in the resurrection, Revelation has an image of narrative Christus Victor. Thus in both the narrative of Jesus from the Gospels and the images of the church in Revelation, the earthly representatives of the reign of God confront the powers of evil—a narrative Christus Victor.

These images of narrative Christus Victor occur at the beginning and end of the New Testament. Between them are the writings of Paul. Writers such as David Brondos, in his book *Paul on the Cross*, make very clear that the writings of Paul fit within these images of narrative Christus Victor.

The relationship of the church to the world changed with Emperor Constantine's adoption of Christianity in the fourth century. The church came to welcome the emperor's support for the church, and eventually Christianity became the only *and* the required religion of the empire. In other words, the church no longer opposed the empire. With the disappearance of that confrontation, the images of Revelation ceased having meaning in the real world. Narrative Christus Victor ceased being a meaningful image.

The narrative Christus Victor of Revelation was largely replaced by the satisfaction image of Anselm of Canterbury, who made the first seminal articulation of it in his 1099 book *Why the God-Man*. Anselm's historical context was feudalism. Stability in society depended on the feudal lord's ability to maintain order. After an offense against the lord disturbed the stability of society, the lord's honor and the stability of society depended on his ability either to exact satisfaction or to punish the offender. Order broke down if the lord could command neither punishment nor satisfaction.

In this context, when Anselm imagined an atonement image, he pictured God as the ultimate feudal lord. Human sin offended God and disturbed the order in the universe. To restore order, satisfaction was required. Since sinful, finite humans could not supply that satisfaction, God sent Jesus as the infinite, sinless God-man to die to supply satisfaction demanded by God's honor and to restore order in the universe. Salvation then depends on identifying with Jesus' death, a saving death that satisfies God's honor.

Notice that in the satisfaction image, there is no necessary role for resurrection. It becomes something else to believe in, located in another section of the theological outline. Note that God is the author of Jesus' death—without death, there is no satisfaction. God sends Jesus to supply the death needed by God's honor. This image also contains the conundrum that the people who kill Jesus both oppose the will of God but also act to give God what God needs, namely an innocent death to satisfy the distorted order in the universe. I agree with feminist writers that this is an image of a God who uses violence and can be argued to

constitute an image of "divine child abuse." Satisfaction atonement has a number of versions. None of the revisions overcomes
these problems.

In response to satisfaction atonement, and in collaboration
with feminists and other contextual writers, *The Nonviolent
Atonement* poses a narrative Christus Victor image that uses the
gospel narrative, writings of Paul, and the book of Revelation.
For ease of reference, I have called this image nonviolent atonement. This version fits the contemporary world and has none of
the problems of the satisfaction image.

Part ***ONE***

PLACING THE PIECES

1

What I Have Always Known and Relearned

Early Years

This narrative recounts what I have learned—and then relearned multiple times—about the things that I always knew. My childhood version of these values included being a peace person and not going to war, being nice to people of color and opposing racism, following the example of Jesus, believing the Bible, and knowing the importance of the church as a witness to the world. Readers can follow the development of adult and mature versions of these beliefs in the story that follows.

I learned my earliest version of these beliefs from two places—my family and our congregation of Argentine Mennonite church, located in the Argentine District of Kansas City, Kansas. The congregation belonged to South Central Conference, which in turn belonged to the Mennonite Church, the largest Mennonite denomination of that epoch. Of course it was many years before I knew anything about these structures beyond our congregation.

Until I was fifteen, my father, mother, younger brother, and I lived in a three-room, basement house, a half mile outside the city limits of Kansas City, Kansas, up a hill at the end of a quarter-mile-long, dead-end road, with only one close neighbor. My father also built a concrete block building to serve as a workshop where he made custom-built furniture for a living. When I was a sophomore in high school, my parents built a much larger, concrete block house on the spot of the basement house, and my father continued to work in his shop until his death. Out here in this relative isolation, where we did not often need to go into town, my parents intended to raise my brother and me without undue influence from "the world."

Our congregation worshipped in a white building, recognizably a church but with no steeple, located two miles from where we lived, on a corner across the street from Stanley school, which I attended from kindergarten through sixth grade. The congregation had perhaps seventy-five members.

Like my parents, most members had grown up in Mennonite congregations in rural areas and were now transplanted to the city. Although my parents did not, many members continued the practice of traditional Mennonite, plain dress. The orientation was both culturally and theologically conservative. We sat on straight benches, men on the left and women on the right, divided by a center aisle. We went to church morning and evening on Sunday, and to prayer meeting on Wednesday evening.

These two entities—isolated family and small, conservative congregation—shaped my early religious outlook. I recall no specific discussions of theology or practice at home. However, I absorbed the sense that the Mennonite church was important, and I took Sunday school learning to heart.

I was religiously sensitive and took seriously the Sunday school teaching that Jesus loved me and could live in my heart. If he lived in my heart, I could go to heaven, which was certainly the goal of all the children in Sunday school. But that presence of Jesus also had an intimidating aspect. Jesus who loved me was always there and watching me; I needed to behave. Jesus knew everything I did, even when I was by myself, and he knew every thought I had, even idle ones or worse. That was a scary proposition. As a child I never got comfortable with Jesus the spy who loved me.

Sitting in the adult church services as a small child, I recall playing with objects my mother made by folding her handkerchief. Later, I played with the fans supplied by a local mortuary, or folded the adult Sunday school papers into boats. Small children met for Sunday school in a rather dank basement. We sat on backless, brown benches and listened to the teacher, my Aunt Martha. In Sunday school I learned that the Bible was the Word of God, a lot of Bible stories, and most importantly, that I was to be a "Jesus boy," which meant following his example. Older children and high school age young people met in classes led by adults, where the discussion content followed the uniform Bible-based lessons published by Herald Press.

I still have my first "Bible," bestowed on me quite early. It is a soft-cover, black volume, two inches high, an inch and a half wide and about three-eighths of an inch thick. The title page identifies it as "The Child's Bible and Prayer Book," by Cecil C. Carpenter. Inside the front cover my mother wrote that it was presented to me on my second Christmas when I would have been twenty-one months old, with a record of my religious development. The story of Jesus is related on ninety-one miniature pages.

Then come two pages for "baby's picture," and my mother dutifully supplied two baby pictures. Then like a big family Bible, there are pages to identify the parents, their wedding date, the doctor and nurse who delivered me. Next come pages where my mother wrote that my favorite book at nineteen months was Egermeier's *Life of Christ*, which I frequently requested to be shown at bedtime. However, most precious of all was this Bible, she wrote, which I took to church and to bed, and used to read about "God, Jesus, and baby Moses." Apparently I have always known that the Bible was important.

When I started kindergarten at Stanley school, I recall feeling that being Mennonite made me different from the other children. A memory that illustrates this sense most clearly comes from the end of that school year, as my class practiced for the May Day festival my grade school put on for parents at the end of the school year. Each class from kindergarten through sixth grade performed a circle dance for the assembled audience.

Such a program required practice. My teacher, Miss Chittenden, took our class of kindergarten children out to the playground for a rehearsal. Circles to guide the dances were painted on the asphalt playground. We practiced our circle dance on these circles, in the shadow of the three-story, red brick school building. I was in the circle of boys, holding the hand of a boy named Donny.

As we moved counter-clockwise, approaching the northeast arc of the circle, Donny and I discussed war. "If you are called you have to go," Donny said.

"No you don't," I replied.

I have no memory of follow-up. At the time, I knew nothing about the provision that was made for religious conscientious objectors to war to do alternative service. I knew only that as a Mennonite and a Jesus boy, I should not go to war.

This conversation with Donny took place in May 1947, two years after the end of World War II in Europe, a bare twenty-one months after the surrender of Japan. I have no memory of discussing the war with my parents, and I knew nothing about Adolf Hitler or concentration camps or the dropping of atomic bombs. What I did know was that Jesus boys did not fight at school and that they did not go to war. Thus at a very young age I was already working on what became a lifelong quest to understand what Jesus' rejection of the sword looks like in the world in which we live.

Some years later I became aware of what was called the Cold War and the threat of nuclear war. When planes flew over our house on the way to the Kansas City Municipal Airport, I often stared up, wondering if any of those planes might have a bomb. From the church ethos I absorbed the idea that the book of Revelation predicted the future. When I learned that the Bible (King James Version) spoke of hornets—likely fused with the locusts with stingers in their tails like scorpions of Revelation 9:7, 10—I got very worried that mention of hornets with stingers was a prediction of planes carrying atomic bombs aimed at us. I discussed that fear with my mother. She said, "I cannot explain why, but we don't believe the Bible that way." I was greatly relieved.

When I was perhaps in fourth grade, my father made what he later said was a mistake. In his workshop he made me a gun that shot rubber loops cut from old inner tubes. I really liked this toy, and I wanted more. I knew how to use the jigsaw and band-saw and hand tools. Reluctantly my father allowed me to make more such guns. Each gun consisted of three pieces of plywood. An inner layer was cut in the shape of a gun, with a space for a trigger, which was a separate piece of wood. Then pieces on the outside were cut on the same pattern of a gun. When fastened together, it became a gun with a trigger to pull that pushed off the rubber band stretched along the barrel. I made one shaped like a rifle and a pair shaped like pistols and then holsters so that I could wear them on a belt.

A spur to making these toy guns was the programs that I listened to on the radio after school. In that time before television, every day through the week there were a series of adventure and cowboy programs—Roy Rogers, Hopalong Cassidy, The Cisco Kid, Sargent Preston of the Yukon, Sky King, Mark Trail. My favorite was The Lone Ranger, which began with the William Tell Overture accompanied by "the thundering hoofbeats" of the Lone Ranger's horse named Silver, gun shots, and his full-throated voice calling "Hi Yo Silver, Away." I tuned in early to make sure that I heard that opening sequence.

As much as I enjoyed these toy guns and these radio shows, I was fully aware of and believed that as a Mennonite I was not to use violence. I knew that my guns were toys, and that I would never use a gun the way the heroes did on the programs that I listened to. I no longer recall how long I kept these toys. Eventually I lost interest and my father was glad to discard them.

As a boy, I knew nothing of the history of slavery in the United States nor of segregation in the South. What I did know very early was that I needed to be nice to Black people. In 1946 or '47, James Lark, only the second African-American Mennonite ordained as a bishop, and his wife Rowena, visited our Argentine Mennonite church in Kansas City. At the time, the Larks were engaged full time in Mennonite mission work among African-Americans in Chicago. When they spoke at our church, my family chauffeured them around in our 1937 Plymouth.

The Larks were my first exposure to African-Americans. I was sitting in the back seat behind my father who was driving, with Rowena in the middle and James by the other window. In the relatively crowded seat, James lay his arm behind Rowena, along the seat back. I eyed his brown hand. My curiosity was aroused, and I could not resist. I sneaked my six-year-old hand up to the seat back, extended my pointer finger, and touched the back of his hand. James felt my touch. He turned to me, and our eyes met. I withdrew my hand and looked away. His look seemed to convey that he recognized my curiosity and thought that I should have known better. I was embarrassed. Thus began my contact with African-Americans, a connection that many years hence would end in a wholehearted embrace of Black Theology.

High School

By the time of my freshman year at Argentine High School in fall 1955, I had embraced the idea that my church's peace stance was "nonresistance." That stance was based on Matthew 5:39, which commanded in the King James Version "that ye resist not evil." The following injunctions about turning the other cheek, giving the cloak with the coat, and going the second mile were given passive interpretations against any kind of protest. At that point I had learned that being a peace person meant not only not going to war, it also meant that I would refuse to fight at school (I never did) and that I would offer no resistance or protest if attacked (I was never attacked).

This understanding of nonresistance shaped my attitude toward the Civil Rights Movement. As the product of a family and a church that had little engagement with society, I knew that I was to be nice to people of color. I knew that Black people experienced discrimination, but I had little awareness of what that discrimination might look like, or of the reality of Jim Crow segregation. I knew that there was a high school in Kansas City for Black students, but that just seemed a normal occurrence. I was unaware of *Brown v. Board of Education*, the ruling handed down 17 May 1954. I did not know the name of Rosa Parks nor did I have any awareness of the Montgomery bus boycott that began in December 1955.

I did know the name of Martin Luther King Jr., but in a less than favorable light. The idea of nonresistance meant just that, no resistance. What I knew was that Martin Luther King Jr. and his civil rights protests were resistance. Thus I, along with my Mennonite church, would never have participated in a public protest. Such activity, we believed, would have violated the command of Jesus "that ye resist not evil." I could accept that African-Americans might be experiencing discrimination, but if they were true followers of Jesus, I believed, they would just have to endure it and not resist the evil. I could even envision that it was not fair that African-Americans might have to suffer more than I did—but that was just the cost of following Jesus.

Until I was in high school I had not gone to school with African-Americans. With my sophomore year in fall 1956, two years after *Brown v. Board of Education*, African-Americans began attending Argentine High School. As far as I knew this integration came off smoothly, but I have no idea how it really went for the African-Americans. I knew only that I was supposed to treat African-Americans with respect. In what now embarrasses me, I also made no move to welcome or befriend or engage with any of the African-Americans at Argentine.

I recall one interaction. During my senior year when I was editor of the school paper, I took a car load of other journalism students to an event at another school. One member of my carload was an African-American woman. After the meeting, as I dropped students off at their homes, it became evident that the last one in the car with me would be the lone African-American woman. She happened to be sitting in the back seat. I was nervous and very self-conscious, unsure what I should say or do.

I had no clarity about the kaleidoscope of feelings that might have been running through her mind. Was she thinking that I should invite her to the front seat, or anxious, or afraid of what I might say or do? Meanwhile, I was uncomfortable with being alone in the car with her. I could have invited her to the front seat, but I said nothing other than to verify where she lived. I think that I retained at least a semblance of nonchalance until I could let her out of the car. In later years, in my interactions with authors of black and womanist theology, this uncomfortable episode sat in the back of my mind.

It was years before I first learned about "white privilege." I can now see that white privilege was an additional dimension of these early beliefs about opposition to Civil Rights protests and the assumption that African-Americans should suffer discrimination as the price of following Jesus. At the time, I had no idea of the advantage white privilege gave me when Argentine High School was integrated, nor the advantage I likely enjoyed in later applications to graduate school. Once I learned about white privilege, dealing with it has become a life-long process.

The interpretation of nonresistance from Matthew 5:39 reflected the understanding of the Bible I inherited from my Mennonite congregation. It was a literalist approach but not fully fundamentalist. The Bible functioned as our rule book. I was aware that 2 Timothy 3:16 said that all Scripture "is given by inspiration of God," which meant that it was all true. However, we did not emphasize that point as fundamentalists did. For us, it was a matter of accepting what the Bible said. Thus nonresistance and not making a response to evil was understood as a teaching of Jesus which Christians ought to obey.

Nonresistance was the most important biblical teaching to be obeyed, but there were others. A significant series of commands came in 1 Corinthians 11. Since man was called the head of the woman (v. 3), all preachers and other church leaders were men. Because Paul wrote that a woman dishonored her head if she prayed with it uncovered (v. 5), all the women in our congregation wore a little white cap, called a covering, when they attended worship. Since a woman's long hair was called "a glory to her," while long hair on a man was "a shame unto him" (vv. 14-15), all men regularly got haircuts while the women all had uncut hair but wore it rolled up in a bun that fit under the covering.

Further, on the basis of Deuteronomy 22:5, which said "the woman shall not wear that which pertaineth unto a man," my mother and the girl that I liked would not wear pants. Since Ephesians 5:19 mentioned "singing and making melody in your heart to the Lord," that meant singing without instruments; thus all singing in our congregation was a cappella. The statement in 1 Peter 33 that the adornment of a wife would "not be that outward adorning of plaiting the hair, and of wearing of gold, or of putting on of apparel," meant that my mother should not wear a wedding ring and that I never bought a class ring.

These cultural practices—male leadership, prayer coverings for women, regulation on women's dress and hair, only a cappella music in church, and opposition to jewelry—were not unique to the congregation in which I grew up; these were the majority views in the Mennonite Church, the national Mennonite denomination to which our Argentine congregation belonged. Within a few decades, these cultural manifestations were largely abandoned. I list them here to illustrate the approach to the Bible with which I grew up.

The literalist approach to the Bible extended beyond these particular Mennonite cultural norms to address an issue of science. I learned a straightforward reading of Genesis 1, with creation taking place in 6 days in 4004 B.C. I verified the date as it was given at the top of the center column reference in my Bible. Of course, opposition to evolution was a given with that outlook. At that time, I knew little or nothing about the multitude of problems with that view, both scientific and textual. I knew only that I believed the Bible, which meant that I rejected the idea of evolution. As a sophomore in high school, I took biology.

One day as we stood by the lab table where we had been dissecting a frog, the teacher, Mr. Hoover, asked me if evolution "bothered my faith." "Yes, sir," I replied. "It doesn't bother mine," Mr. Hoover countered. I knew that Mr. Hoover attended the Methodist church located one block away from my Mennonite church. To my mind, I had made a "witness" about true, biblical faith to liberal Mr. Hoover.

By the time I entered high school, I had come to love and enjoy mathematics. Algebra made sense, and at the end of the year I made the highest score on the standardized test in our school. Later I learned that I had also topped scores in the other large city high school. Moving to plane geometry the next year, to Algebra II as a junior, and to solid geometry and trigonometry as a senior were all natural moves. Mathematics was a discipline that pursued problems until answers emerged. I relished every minute of it.

The discipline of mathematics was accompanied by an attitude that in our twenty-first-century context has been exposed as unacceptable. As I moved through the sequence of courses there was an apparent winnowing of people who could do math, a winnowing that seemed normal at the time. For ninth grade algebra, there were two classes, about evenly divided between boys and girls. The next year, there was one class of plane geometry, with more boys than girls. By Algebra II in my junior year, only three girls remained, and they sat over by the windows, while the dozen or so eager boys—the "real" students—sat in the middle of the room in front of Doc Shell, the teacher. The final year, no girls took solid geometry and trigonometry—and that appeared normal to me.

I emerged from this experience in high school firmly committed to being a math major in college. It was several years before I learned terms like *patriarchy* and *male dominance* and realized how objectionable that worldview was. Nothing of this scenario portended my later, sometimes uncomfortable, learning about the importance of listening to women's voices, nor the women who would one day praise my construction of atonement theology.

A world-shaking event also materially impacted my decision to study math and science (although I was not nearly as interested in chemistry as in mathematics). In my junior year of high school, on 4 October 1957, the Soviet Union caught the western world by surprise with the launch of Sputnik, the world's first artificial earth satellite. Occurring amid the Cold War, this hint of possible scientific and military superiority by the major Cold War adversary of the United States sent a chill through American society. Despite the relative isolation I shared with my church and family, I felt that fear myself.

As I recall, there was a sense that the U.S. education system was soft and had to do a better job of producing scientists and engineers. A clear sense soon emerged that good students should study math and science to produce more scientists and engineers to build rockets to beat the feared Russians. I was not interested in building rockets. But as one of the good students, I was willing to ride the wave of interest in mathematics and science into college. After all, it was a discipline for smart students. It was several years before I learned that "smart people"—women as well as men—studied disciplines other than science and math.

I finished high school as a biblical literalist, firmly committed to nonresistance, a believer in male headship and patriarchy, and committed to studying mathematics as the discipline for "smart people."

I had no idea how much college would challenge and reorient my thinking.

2

Too Much Fun

I began my college education in fall 1959, at Hesston College, a small Mennonite, junior college in Hesston, Kansas. I was still under the influence of the Sputnik scare, still fully committed to pursuing my love of mathematics, with a probable future career as a math teacher. When it came to discussing potential areas of study, I made no effort to explore anything else. If any counselor attempted to entice me to explore additional areas as well, I do not recall—regardless, it would have fallen on deaf ears. Nonetheless, although I had no idea of its import at the time, I did encounter a subject area that would eventually become one dimension of my entire academic career. Meanwhile, I had a lot of fun at Hesston.

For starters, I played all the intramural sports, served as a statistician for the men's basketball team, and played first base and catcher on the baseball team. Life in the dorm had endless delights—the frequent bull sessions, the Rook games, learning to play Canasta and draw poker with popcorn kernels, and general playing around.

One prank remains a vivid memory. The two men who lived next door invited me in on an escapade to steal the spoons from the dining hall. The deed took planning. It would be necessary to hide the container of spoons in a location where they would be found after enough time for the deed to be fully acknowledged but before the administration got really annoyed and took action.

The heist was carried out the day before a major program, and the container of spoons hidden with the chairs that would be set up for that program. The night of the prank, I put my paja-mas on, took my toothbrush with toothpaste and walked around in the hall, making sure that I was seen by our hall manager, who was studying in the lobby. I got in bed at the same time as my roommate and we doused the lights. I waited for my roommate to fall asleep, and then I crept quietly out of our room and went next door. I dressed in the clothes that I had previously de-posited there.

With the hall manager still studying in the lobby at the other end, we sneaked down the hall, exited the building, and crossed campus to the gym, which housed the cafeteria in the basement. We managed to pry open a window in the underground cafete-ria, crawl through, find the big pan of spoons, and take it up-stairs and hide it under the stage with the folding chairs that would be set up a day later on the gym floor.

No one saw our trek back to the dorm, and I climbed into my bed without waking my roommate. Since my roommate and I were both involved in many activities, both formal and informal, we were natural suspects. But when queried, I would turn to my roommate and say, "Hey Calvin, they think we stole the spoons." And Calvin would say, "No, Denny went to bed when I did last night." The hall manager also vouched for me, saying that he had seen me ready for bed. If my roommate and the hall man-ager read this account, they will learn for the first time how they became unwitting accomplices.

I did have a good time, probably too good a time, at Hesston. In fact I had so much fun that it was not always apparent I in-tended to get an education. In one evening bull session, there had been discussion of guys who were not serious about college; the speaker listed my name among others on this nefarious list.

I laughed along with everyone else, but inside I was embar-rassed and chastened. I wanted to be recognized as a good stu-dent. I did well in pre-calculus, then calculus, followed by differential equations. In fact, I received the Chemical Rubber Company handbook of mathematical tables that was given to the outstanding Freshman math student. In those days before scientific hand calculators, this handbook was the indispensable tool for mathematicians.

I also recall my conduct in one course in which I was anything but the image of the good student that I wanted to project. The professor lectured in a monotone and the content did not grab my interest. One day, I heard a name mentioned several times. Since I had not been following the lecture, I had no idea that the named individual was the focus of the entire class session. In a misguided effort to show interest, I raised my hand and asked, "Who is Bismarck?" The shocked professor did not answer my question. Instead he said, "Please come to my office after class." I appeared in his office, and he asked, "Was that an honest question?" I admitted that I really did not know who Bismarck was. I do not recall our further conversation. Only later did I realize how really rude and out of line my question was.

Meanwhile, there was also the way that I treated the course. For the first test, my hallmates and I were worried, and we studied hard. I received an A on the multiple choice test. On the next test I received an A-. I got more and more lackadaisical, and my grade declined on each successive test. The professor had displayed the formula that included all tests in determining the final grade. I calculated that if I scored an F on the final exam, my average for the course would be C+. Thus I did no studying at all for the final. I guessed at a D minus rating, and received a B minus for the course. Looking back, my professorial self is not impressed with Denny the student.

The course whose long-term implications I did not suspect was an introduction to church history, taught by Gideon G. Yoder, known familiarly as Gid Yoder. He was married to the younger sister of my grandmother Elsie Beyler, who had died of Spanish flu in 1920, when my mother was five years old. Thus I called him Uncle Gid. Uncle Gid laughed a lot and spoke with a slight rasp. He was a short, full-bodied man, bald with a round face. He wore a black suit to class with white shirt, often without a tie. Always a bit rumpled, his coat had a perpetual white streak from where he leaned against the chalk tray.

Uncle Gid introduced me to Anabaptist history, the movement from which Mennonites are descended. I sat in the front row with one of my friends. We learned that Anabaptism emerged as an exciting movement in the sixteenth-century Reformation, and that its meaning for us was to get involved in the church. He drew a circle on the blackboard, taped the chalk in the middle of it and said that we should "get involved." "Involved" was a paradigmatic word for Uncle Gid, and we watched for it. Once he stopped himself in mid-sentence and said, "I was just about to say 'involved' but these guys in the front row get too big a kick out of it." We loved Uncle Gid. I had no idea that fifteen years later I would look at this class as the beginning of one of my career-long pursuits.

Gideon Yoder died in 1971, when I was in graduate school studying Anabaptist history. Since I was visiting my parents in Kansas City at the time, I drove out to Hesston and gave a tribute at his funeral. I identified his class as the event that first sparked my interest in Anabaptism. I dedicated *Becoming Anabaptist*, my first book, to his memory.

There was other foreshadowing in Gideon Yoder's class as well. He spoke of the "Elkhart Team" of John F. Funk and John S. Coffman and the "Goshen Team" of Harold S. Bender and John C. Wenger. Funk was perhaps the outstanding leader of the Mennonite Church in the nineteenth century. He owned the Mennonite Publishing Company in Elkhart, Indiana, and published the influential Mennonite periodical *Herold der Wahrheit/Herald of Truth*. Coffman was Funk's younger collaborator, assistant editor, and frequent contributor to the periodical until his untimely death in 1899.

Bender was the widely respected dean of the Mennonite seminary in Goshen, Indiana, and had written the well-known essay "The Anabaptist Vision," which defined the paradigm of Anabaptism for the two decades since its publication in 1943. Wenger was an esteemed churchman and professor of Anabaptist history at the seminary who saw his role as the popularizer of Bender's "Anabaptist Vision."

As I heard these names in Uncle Gid's class, it was beyond my imagination that within twenty years I would be reading the writings of all four of these men and publishing my own analyses of their work. Nor could I envision that by the end of my career, I would be part of what Uncle Gid might have called "the Bluffton Team." And more important than any of the above is the fact that I have been married to Wenger's daughter, Mary Lois, for more than fifty years.

But these last comments are getting ahead of the story. I arrived at Hesston College with my biblical literalist, nonresistant faith, and the intent to study mathematics. I left with these commitments still intact. At Goshen College, I would encounter ideas and people that challenged my basic assumptions and pointed me in a different academic direction.

3

A Goal

I was halfway through my career as a college religion professor before I called myself a theologian, the professional identity I still claim. My path to that identity was neither straight nor smooth. In some cases, it required as much unlearning as learning, both short- and long-term. The first step toward becoming a theologian was the actual decision to become a religion professor. It happened at Goshen College, via some initially uncomfortable learning.

Goshen College is a Mennonite, four-year, liberal arts school in Goshen, Indiana. I arrived there in 1961 after two years at Hesston, with my high school faith and my intention to study mathematics fully intact. I did continue my math major, as well as additional science courses.

But two things happened. One, I got rather bored with mathematics. At that epoch there were not yet any hand-held calculators; we did math on paper with a pencil. The indispensable tool was the CRC math handbook that I had received as a freshman. It was full of tables—logarithms to 5 and 7 figures (usually called logs), log logs, trig functions in minutes and degrees, logs of trig functions, radians, tables of numbers to base e, and much more. We learned the process of interpolation, a way of using the numbers in the log tables to multiply huge numbers, and otherwise manipulate figures and find values in between the numbers in the tables. Today these figures all reside in a hand-held, scientific calculator, and the answers are quickly available with a few touches of the key pad. At that time, however, it might require twenty minutes of pencil work that covered an entire sheet of paper to arrive at an answer.

After a while, it seemed to me that such processes had little meaning beyond figures on paper, and I was not enjoying the process anymore. Parallel to this development, I was also realizing that I was less interested than I once was in following the course of the carbon or nitrogen atoms in a chemical equation or pouring chemicals into test tubes to determine the identity of an unknown substance.

Second, Norman Kraus happened to me—twice. He stood over six feet tall, slender, with a thin face and wavy hair. He was personable with a ready smile. As a sponsor of the junior class, he made an effort to entertain all junior students in his house in small groups. While he wore a coat and tie to class, the coat did not always match his pants. Norman taught required religion courses at Goshen. One of those courses was Protestant Christianity. Another was American Religion. Norman was one of Goshen's younger faculty, his lectures were scintillating, and he could speak knowledgeably about seemingly anything. But initially I was not enthralled. My first jolt from Norman concerned nonresistance.

A gentle nudge away from or beyond my commitment to nonresistance occurred when I took Guy F. Hershberger's class "War, Peace, and Nonresistance." Guy was a leading voice in peace teaching of that era. His book *The Way of the Cross in Human Relations*, a text for the course, was one of the first pieces of literature for Mennonites to argue that being peace people and a peace church included more than passive nonresistance and refusing to participate in war. Rather, it involved a positive witness for peace. By this time, Guy was nearing the end of his career. I picture him in class in black suit and tie, thin face, no hair on the top of his head, amid the mannerism that so amused us. He frequently removed his glasses and used the ear piece to probe in his ear, and then stood with his mouth open for seconds on end when considering how to answer a question or complete a thought.

We enjoyed this elderly Guy, who taught that nonresistance meant to give a positive witness. An example was the experience he recounted from a trip through the South that he made with a small, racially integrated group of men. On one occasion when they entered a restaurant, Guy related, the waitress informed them that the manager had said that she could serve the white men but not their Black companion. The white men ordered and asked for an extra plate. Guy chuckled as he described how the tittering waitress brought the extra plate and place setting, willingly abetting their plan. When the food arrived, half was transferred to the plate of the Black man, and they ate lunch together. Guy was pleased with this example of positive, nonresistant witness. But for me, still steeped in nonresistance, it was rather far out. I turned to the friend seated next to me and said, "Ole Guy went too far." The friend agreed.

A vigorous push away from nonresistance came from Norman Kraus. Before I had taken any classes with Norman, I sat in the Sunday school class he taught for college students. He had just finished his doctoral degree at Duke University in Durham, North Carolina, where he had been exposed to the lunch counter sit-ins.

This movement began on February 1, 1960, in nearby Greensboro when four Black students from North Carolina A and T sat down at a segregated lunch counter at the Woolworth's store downtown. When service was refused, they remained seated the rest of the day. More students joined in following days, and by February 5, three hundred students crowded into the Woolworth's. The practice of sit-ins soon spread across the south and into the north.

In the Sunday school class, Norman reported on and supported the lunch counter sit-ins and other civil rights protests. For me, who had long assumed that nonresistance meant "no resistance," and thus that civil rights protests were resisting, this was heady and even threatening material. It seemed that Norman Kraus was abandoning the sacred teaching of Jesus about "nonresistance."

It took awhile, but under Norman's influence I came to accept the validity of civil rights protests, even for nonresistant Mennonites. Beginning to develop an understanding of peace teaching and peace practice that moved beyond nonresistance is the first debt I owe to Norman Kraus. It was gratifying a number of years later to be able to thank Norman in a public setting for first moving me beyond nonresistance.

The second specific challenge from Norman concerned evolution. I carried the belief learned from my church of creation in six days in 4004 B.C. into Norman's course on American religion. Norman lectured on the origin of evolution, and the controversy about its acceptance in nineteenth- and twentieth-century America. Norman was not advocating the theory of evolution, but he gave it a fair hearing in a historical context. Hearing a supposed biblical absolute placed in its historically relative context was threatening. I was shocked. Back in Shoup House, the student house where I lived, I expressed my horror that Norman Kraus "believed in evolution."

Perry Yoder and Gene Stoltzfus, students at Goshen Biblical Seminary on the edge of the college campus, also lived in Shoup House. They heard my denunciation of Norman. Perry and Gene sat me down in our lobby, and in no uncertain terms showed me where I was wrong and what I needed to learn. They explained that the Genesis accounts of creation were not to be read as scientific statements about how creation occurred, but rather as poetic statements with theological meaning. We could thus accept evolution as a scientific theory without a sense that it contradicted the theological statements of the Bible. I thought about it for a couple days and realized that Perry and Gene were correct. I was relieved about Norman, I was soon one of his fans, and my real theological education had begun.

Many years later I had occasion to tell Norman what had happened to me in his course. I asked if he had intended that kind of response. He assured me that he had. In the church constituency at that time, he explained, there were still a lot of folks who opposed evolution. Because advocating evolution was politically fraught, he had to approach it indirectly. His approach was certainly effective for me. I thanked him for it.

I idolized professors like Norman, who could answer questions knowledgeably about virtually any topic. Another such paragon of seemingly infinite wisdom was history professor John Oyer. In appearance he was the stereotypical college professor, average build, thinning hair, proper of speech, well-dressed in conservative brown suit and dark tie. I took one course with John, listened to him speak in our twice weekly forums, and hung around groups where I could hear him discourse informally.

On one occasion, John Oyer hosted John Brademas, a representative from the Indiana district that included Goshen to the Congress in Washington, D.C. Oyer introduced Brademas in forum. After the presentation, Oyer asked him a question. Representative Brademas was rendered speechless; he gulped and had no answer. Oyer's performance had me in awe—he had stumped a United States Congressman! I do not recall the question, but it would have concerned political science and current policy. Many years later, I had occasion to ask John Oyer if he remembered the moment or his question. He had no recollection of it.

As I drifted away from math and science and decided on a career as a religion professor, Norman Kraus and John Oyer were my models. I wanted to be like them, to be able to answer any question, to appear to know everything.

Other learnings had less immediate academic impetus. One concerned crisis conversions. From the back bench during a revival meeting at Argentine Mennonite Church, I raised my hand in a revival meeting. I was nine years old and received baptism a few Sundays later after instruction class taught by the minister. At age fifteen, "just to be sure" that I was saved, I raised my hand in response to the invitation at a Youth For Christ rally. Although the memory is fuzzy, I think that I also raised my hand in a meeting at Hesston College.

But without undergoing any crisis of faith or weighty conversations with a pastor, I came to the realization that I did not need this kind of emotional impulse to validate my commitment to Christian faith and more particularly to the Jesus who lived the example of nonviolence. Although it was a number of years before I could articulate it this way, I came to understand that whether studying the Bible, Anabaptist or church history, or theology, I was continually affirming my commitment as a disciple of Jesus.

I graduated from college in spring 1963 listed as a math major. I was also close to qualifying as a religion major. I enrolled in the seminary adjacent to the college campus, and embarked on what would become an eleven-year odyssey until I first stood in front of a classroom as a professor of religion. I had no idea how much I would learn, nor of the changes in direction still to come.

4

Bible Scholar

In the fall of 1963, I walked across an expanse of grass and a driveway and enrolled in Goshen Biblical Seminary, one half of Associated Mennonite Biblical Seminaries (hereafter AMBS and renamed Anabaptist Mennonite Biblical Seminary as of 2012). With no second thoughts about abandoning mathematics, I was embarking on what eventually became an eleven-year trek through seminary and graduate school with a four-year interlude for service abroad, culminating in a career as a professor of an area of Bible, theology, or church history yet to be determined. I had little understanding of the potential pitfalls of such a plan; I knew only that it was what I wanted to do. In this stint in seminary, I collected a wealth of important data that would serve me well in future academic endeavors, and decided on a graduate school specialty—a decision that held for several years.

I took the standard seminary curriculum. For the New Testament, I studied Greek. I was excited to make my own translation of the gospel of John, our assignment in first-year Greek. In New Testament survey, I learned about the synoptic problem—the question of how to understand the relationship of Matthew, Mark, and Luke, who differed in details while having significant common material. For Old Testament I took Old Testament survey, several courses on writings of the Prophets, and studied Hebrew, the language of the Old Testament.

Of these courses, the material that resonated the most was the Old Testament and the Hebrew language. Millard Lind was the professor who animated this learning. He was short, with round face and thinning hair, and clad in a black suit with no tie. His quiet voice, tending toward the tenor, coupled with his obvious love of the material, pulled me into the Old Testament.

From Millard, I realized for the first time that the Old Testament was not merely a collection of random sayings, writings, and stories. It actually contained a long running narrative with a plot. The story began with the call of Abraham, and continues with his descendants who become the Children of Israel. They experienced enslavement in Egypt, a dramatic escape, a period of wandering in the wilderness, occupation of Palestine, rule by judges and then by kings, the division of the kingdom, defeat and exile in Babylon, and return from exile. In the New Testament, Jesus is a continuation of this story.

I was captivated by the fact that the writings of the Prophets were commentary on the conduct of the kings and other leaders of Israel, often a commentary that challenged greed and corruption. These prophets did talk about the future, but it was not predictions of the future in a way that was beyond normal human ability to know. The Prophets based their statements on their reading of the political situation.

For example, Isaiah walked around Jerusalem naked for three years in anticipation of the coming military defeat and shame of Egypt and Ethiopia being led away captive, and including Israel that wanted to make an alliance with them. The actions of Ezekiel, a prophet of the Babylonian exile, may strike us as crazy. He drew Jerusalem on a brick and lay speechless on his side around the brick and ate siege rations for 430 days, the traditional number of years of the Israelites in Egypt, thus bearing in his body their suffering in defeat and captivity.

A most striking example of a prophet's reading of the times appeared in Millard's analysis of the book of Jeremiah. Several times Jeremiah wrote that punishment—an invasion of Israel—would come "out of the north" (1:4; 4:6; 6:1, 22; 10:22). Millard explained that with desert to the east of Israel, invasions only came from the direction of Egypt in the south, or one of the powers to the north. The statement of invasion from the north, Millard continued, came after the battle of Carchemish in 605 B.C., when Egypt was defeated by armies from the north, who would then attack Israel. Then in 20:4, Jeremiah wrote that Judah will be given into the hand of the king of Babylon. This more specific pronouncement, Millard explained, followed a battle between Assyria and Babylon, in which Babylon emerged the victor. Finally in 21:1-2 came the most specific statement of all: it will be the Babylonian king Nebuchadnezzar who leads the invasion. There had been a dynastic struggle in Babylon, and when Nebuchadnezzar won, Jeremiah could then give his name as the one who will lead the destruction from the north. Jeremiah was anticipating the defeat of Judah and captivity in Babylon that arrived in 587 B.C.

With such analysis of Isaiah, Ezekiel, and Jeremiah, Millard Lind explained the function of the modern prophet. It was not to copy the biblical prophets, some of whose actions were decidedly deranged, but to provide commentary on events occurring in the present.

Beyond this fascinating material from the biblical text, there was the Hebrew language. It was exotic, with its right to left orientation and letters not derived from any letters I had previously known. Coming to see that these letters made words that I could understand, and that I could begin to read the Old Testament in the original language, stimulated me greatly. I wrote vocabulary words and verb paradigms on cards and memorized them religiously (pun intended!).

One semester-long assignment was to read the book of Jonah in Hebrew. With Millard's enthusiasm and the scintillating material in the text, what was not to like about studying the Old Testament? It was a thrill to be able to read in the original language that appeared so different from English. Some colleagues responded differently, complaining about having to learn a dead language. As we left a final exam, I heard someone yell, "Now we can forget our Hebrew." But for me, with a grasp of all the verb forms in the book, sitting in a circle and reading Jonah with Millard's encouragement was not only educational but enjoyable! By the end of two years in seminary, I had found my direction. I would attend graduate school in Old Testament and become a professor of Old Testament.

Meanwhile, in the world beyond seminary, the war in Vietnam continued to escalate. As a seminary student, I was deferred from the draft. However, I was not satisfied merely to avoid service. I wanted some kind of involvement, and I wanted an experience outside of the United States. I changed my draft classification to 1-O, the classification for Conscientious Objectors available for alternative service.

With fiancée Mary Lois Wenger, we volunteered for a term of service with Mennonite Central Committee. Since I would no longer be in seminary, this would be service that was the alternative to military service. In June 1965 Mary graduated from Goshen College in the morning with a degree in nursing. We were married that evening. I have not written her into this narrative, but Mary is and remains the center of my life, and lived the story to follow with me.

A few days later, we began a summer course in French at Goshen College. That fall we left the United States for a three-year term with Mennonite Central Committee—language study in Brussels, Belgium and then a posting to Algeria in north Africa. My future goal of being a professor of Old Testament was firmly in place. But challenging times lay ahead.

5

Becoming
Another Person

In late summer of 1965, Mary and I arrived in Brussels, Belgium, ready to begin serious study of French. We were part of a Mennonite Central Committee contingent who would learn French in preparation for assignment in a French-speaking country. The ultimate goal for Mary and me was Algeria. Along with all kinds of learnings from our first time abroad, acquiring facility in French was the exciting and most visible result of living in Brussels. It served me well in later aspects of my career. An unexpected revelation about Christian faith, quite apart from learning French, also had long term career impact.

We lived in two rooms of an apartment owned by Madame Williems, a widowed, retired theater actress. We called her "Madame." It was expected that each evening we would watch Belgium television with Madame and practice our French. One of our favorite shows was "Le Saint," which we learned appeared on American TV as "The Saint."

We were enrolled in L'École d'Administration, a school that provided French language instruction for missionaries and other practitioners headed for Belgium's recently independent colony, the Congo. On the first day of class, we made the short walk from our rooms on Rue Gachard up the hill to Avenue Louise, where we entered a large building.

We found our classroom, took seats, and surveyed the room. I was unprepared for what I saw. There were perhaps 60 prospective French learners. In front of us on the left side of the center aisle, the first two rows were occupied by men in clerical coats—Catholic priests that we soon learned were Italian. The first two rows on the right side of the aisle were occupied by women in religious habits—nuns that we learned were from Spain. This was the most Catholics I had shared space with since the time in high school my violin quartet played for a PTO meeting at a Catholic school—and that was the first and only other time I had been in a room with so many Catholics. These Catholics now comprised about half the French class, and the rest included a variety of students from the United States, a number from England, and a couple from Australia.

To fully portray the impact—even the shock—of my seeing these rows of Catholic religious, a couple of anecdotes may be helpful. I do not recall hearing anti-Catholic sentiment expressed at church. Neither do I recall anti-Catholic conversations at home during my growing up years. But I certainly absorbed the anti-Catholic ethos of 1950's America and of Mennonites as well.

Back when my high school violin quartet received the invitation to perform for the PTO meeting in a Catholic school, I had to consider whether I should go—deigning to play for Catholics might be tantamount to approving their religion, and what little I knew about Catholics was that they were wrong. But I did go and we set up our music stands and prepared to play. My skin felt kind of creepy, just being in the parish church where the PTO met. The sisters who taught at the school were seated in front. When the priest appeared, everyone stood, quickly recited a prayer, and crossed themselves at its conclusion. It sounded like mumbling to my skeptical ears, and I refused to bow my head. We played, and immediately afterward, I escaped outside, glad to be liberated from such a wrong-headed place.

Later, as a sophomore at Hesston College during the 1960 presidential election that pitted John F. Kennedy against Richard M. Nixon, naturally I supported Richard Nixon. I did not want the pope telling the United States president what to do. With some friends, we went to nearby Newton and found the local Republican campaign headquarters. We picked up some

Nixon campaign literature, including a Nixon bumper sticker, which I proudly posted on the bulletin board in my dorm room. My parents had a tradition of sending family picture Christmas cards. That Christmas, their card included a picture of me, sitting at my desk with the Nixon bumper sticker clearly in view. Years later, my aunts, knowing that I had repented of my earlier political leanings, would tease me about the "Nixon picture."

These anecdotes describe the outlook that I carried into the French class in Brussels, where I discovered my Catholic classmates. My response? Here would be my first opportunity to show Catholics how wrong they were. My education was about to begin.

I was oblivious to the fact that Vatican II had been underway since 1962 and was drawing near its conclusion that December. This first council in a century for the Catholic Church was initiating great changes. These included the promulgation the previous year of the decree *Unitatis redintegratio*, which elevated non-Catholics from schismatic heretics to the status of "separated Christian brethren." Of course, the Catholics in our French class knew about these exciting developments. Never before had they had access to so many Protestants. While I was eager to show them how wrong they were, they were eager to build relationships with their "separated brethren."

To the extent that my improving French allowed, I did engage with the priests. True to my intent, I began by seeking disagreements where I could prove them wrong. But they challenged me: "Don't look for disagreements. Let's look for things we can agree on." Although I was as yet unaware of it, they were acting on the "brethren" rather than the "separated" element of separated brethren and had fully abandoned the earlier schismatic designation. To have time for a more fruitful conversation than our class time tea breaks allowed, the priests invited me to come for a Bible study at the monastery where they were staying.

The Bible study proved interesting and revelatory, though I no longer recall any details. I suspect that we read a Gospel. I know that their suggestion was to read the text and then to make statements that we could agree on. It did not take long for me to learn that I really could read the Bible with these priests. I learned that they were indeed my "Christian brethren." After this encounter, I enjoyed our daily interactions at French class. I even expanded my stamp collection by trading stamps with one of the Spanish nuns.

Learning to accept Catholics as Christians that I did not need to convert was an experience that had a long-lasting and wide-ranging impact on my life and career. Most immediately, it opened the way for us to be an accepted part of the small Catholic community in Al-Asnam when we got to Algeria in 1966. It shaped my conversation when I met a cardinal. But that is another story.

Meanwhile, after our school year of formal French study concluded, we had one additional opportunity to practice French before we traveled to Algeria. We spent the summer at la Villa des Sapins, a children's home managed by French Mennonites at Valdoie, near Belfort in the Alsace region of France. It was an excellent opportunity to be immersed in French language, engaging with children and helping the staff with maintenance and daily tasks. In terms of long-term impact, we gained a view of Mennonites in France.

By the time we left France, I enjoyed using my new facility with French in a variety of settings. It was particularly satisfying to handle an interaction in French, such as in a bank where the teller certainly knew English and finish my business without having the teller switch to English. Sometimes it was like I had become another person, as I stood watching this American man I knew speak French. I have never gotten over that thrill of functioning well in another language.

We enjoyed our summer in France. It felt like a culture quite close to our own, except for the language. By the end of summer, we were ready to move on to Algeria, where we would meet a culture quite different from our own.

6

Algeria

Our journey to Algeria consisted of a train ride from Belfort to Marseilles and then a boat trip across the Mediterranean Sea to Algiers, the capital. After a few days in Algiers with the Mennonite Central Committee director for Algeria, we took the train to Al-Asnam (recently renamed Chlef), a city of some 40,000 located about 130 miles west of Algiers, where we would live for the next two years. We learned much in that time, learning that would have a material impact on my theological understanding and career direction as well as political outlook.

Living in Algeria was our first direct and personal encounter with colonialism. It began on our journey to Algeria. At the dock in Marseilles, we got in line behind a long queue of Algerians waiting to board our boat from the south of France to the north of Algeria. A French official tapped me on the shoulder and motioned that we should follow him. He took us to the front of the line and checked us in. We were caught up in and submitted passively to what I now identify as the white privilege of those who look like the colonial occupier.

I soon learned a bit of Algerian history. Under French colonial rule, Algeria was governed as a department of France. However, the native Muslim Algerians were considered second-class citizens. For example, their passports read French-Algeria, in contrast to the native European Algerians or *Pieds-noir* (black feet), whose passports identified them as French.

After more than a century of French colonial rule, in 1954 the Front de Libération Nationale (FLN) began a guerrilla war against France. France responded with harsh reprisals and torture. The Algerians suffered tens of thousands of casualties. After a series of upheavals in the French government, the newly installed President Charles de Gaulle recognized the war was unwinnable by France. In 1959, he offered Algeria independence, and complex negotiations were opened with the FLN. Algeria was granted complete independence in 1962. The *Pieds-noir*, who had opposed an independent Algeria, feared reprisals from Algerians. Nine hundred thousand *Pieds-noir* fled to France after independence.

When we arrived in late summer of 1966, Algerians were still enjoying the first blush of political independence. Our new friends talked readily about how their war had defeated France. Their newly gained independence depended on that war. We fought and won, they said. Our young neighbor told a story about the nefarious conduct of the French military. On the edge of town near our apartment building was a concrete structure in a traffic island. French soldiers propped dead Algerian guerrillas against this structure, our new friend explained, with a sign that said, "We will not launch any more grenades."

I had the nonresistant belief with which I had grown up in mind, as I observed the Algerians' obvious joy at independence as well as listened to the stories of our young neighbor. If I had any lingering doubt about abandoning nonresistance after the push from Norman Kraus, hearing these accounts in Algeria removed any last doubts. For these Algerians, a supposed witness to the truth of Jesus Christ by refusing to fight and submitting to continued domination by the French colonial administration would have been meaningless as well as nonsensical. I realized that if a Christian peace witness, or Jesus' rejection of the sword, was to have any meaning in their revolutionary context, it had to go beyond nonresistance, beyond not responding to evil. It had to engage in some kind of nonviolent activism that would challenge and attempt to change a violent and unjust situation.

In Al-Asnam, I was assigned to teach English in the town's lycée Es-Salem, or Es-Salem high school. The main structure of the school consisted of a large courtyard surrounded by classrooms on three sides, and service rooms on the fourth. One room on the corner of the courtyard contained the office for the dean of students, who oversaw daily activity of the school. Also nearby was the office for the *Proviseur*, or principal, and other administrators. There were multiple sections of each grade, from about freshmen to seniors. Each section of each grade was assigned to a specific room and the teachers moved from room to room throughout the school day. When the bell sounded, students got up from their desks, exited the room, and lined up outside in front of their room, and waited for the next teacher to arrive and give them permission to enter.

The lycée operated on the inherited French system and still reflected French influence. The faculty consisted largely of French people, many of whom were French military or their spouses. Men could avoid the required French military service by spending eighteen months teaching in Algeria. Men from Palestine, Syria, or Egypt, who knew little French, taught classical Arabic. I was an English teacher, alongside a French woman who also taught English.

I was an inexperienced teacher, to say the least. I had had no education classes in college and had never before stood in front of a class. It was assumed that I knew what to do, but I was dropped into lycée Es-Salem with no introduction to the French system or its ethos beyond the list of the classes to which I was assigned. I arrived for the first day of class and observed several hundred students milling around in the courtyard. I had no idea where my rooms would be. A teacher I asked for help pointed and said "Over there." When the bell sounded, and students lined up in front of their classrooms, I started down the line and asked each class if they were the one for which I was looking. With big smiles, they said "yes," but so did the class next to them! Testing the rookie teacher was indeed fun.

Eventually I did find my class and gave the sign for them to enter. I stepped into the room and learned my next lesson. Students made a half-hearted effort to stand when I followed them into the room, but I indicated that standing was not necessary for me. The noise in the room increased exponentially. I quickly intuited an important lesson about the French system, namely that the teacher—called a *professeur*—is an authority figure; order in the classroom depended on the authority being able to command the respect of the students. Requiring that they stand quietly until I gave permission for them to sit was the first visible mark of respect that I could command to begin each class period. Maintaining order would be my primary problem for the two years I spent in this school.

I wanted a seating chart so that I could learn the names of the students. Quickly I sketched the rows and columns for forty students. I started at the top of row one and asked for a name. Making a seating chart proved a trying task. With unfamiliar names like Mohammed, Ahmed, Achmed, and Mamoud that sound similar to the uninitiated, particularly against the background of a noisy class, making a seating chart took a while. Eventually, I did have a chart, began to learn names, and could make an effort to accomplish something in a class. Although developing the seating chart had its difficulty, apparently it eventually gained me some good will. A class of forty-six students told me I was the only one of their teachers who knew all their names. But there was still much to learn.

An immediate problem was the lack of chalk and eraser in my classroom. Although other teachers always seemed to have that equipment, on more than one occasion I tried to stretch a centimeter-long piece of chalk through an entire period while erasing with a wadded-up piece of notebook paper.

After several days with minimal chalk and no eraser in my classes, I took matters into my own hands. I went to see the principal and asked for my own eraser that I could carry around with me in my book bag. He gave me a quizzical look, which indicated that it was an unusual request, and suggested that I have a responsible student get it for me. I insisted that I really did want to have my own eraser—if I carried it myself I could always count on having an eraser. The principal granted my request. That he had to search for a while to find an eraser further demonstrated how far my request deviated from normal practice. I thanked him profusely for his efforts and went happily on my way.

The next step was to locate the source of chalk. It turned out to be in the office of the dean of students, located handily on the edge of the courtyard. On my way to class each day, I could drop in and pick up chalk. Again there was mention of having a responsible student pick up chalk, but I explained that I preferred to do it myself so that I could be certain that I would always have chalk. The dean of students agreed. Again I expressed my gratitude and departed happy.

I put my eraser and chalk in a plastic bag and it became a permanent accessory of the book bag I carried to class every day. Never again did I go through a class with a centimeter of chalk and a wad of notebook paper for an eraser. I was delighted with what individual initiative could accomplish in the face of seeming indifference to details and good organization. I was delighted—until I found out what was really happening.

I no longer recall the circumstances, but in the last week of the school year, I learned what I had missed. Blame it on my less-than-perfect understanding of French, along with inattention to possible cultural differences. I had heard something seemingly obvious all year without realizing that my understanding was faulty.

The magic word was *responsible* as in responsible student. In French, the adjective alone became a noun. The principal, the dean of students, and other teachers had mentioned "le responsable de classe," for which a literal English translation sounds like "the responsible student of the class." When the principal and dean had mentioned having the "responsable de classe" get chalk and eraser, I had presumed that they were simply suggesting that I pick a responsible student and ask that student to get an eraser and chalk for me.

My assumption was quite wrong. In fact, "le responsable de classe" was a technical term. It was the title of an office with specific duties assigned to a student in each class. In our system, we might call this student "the class secretary."

The dean chose the "le responsable de classe" for each class. Among the assigned duties for this student was the job of keeping the eraser for the class and picking up chalk for the *professeur* from the office of the dean. While I spent the year admiring my initiative and efficiency in having chalk and eraser every day, each of my classes of students was secretly laughing at me, enjoying my ignorance of the system, and the fact that I was stooping to do a student's job.

I laughed with the students at my ignorance. They had fooled me, and they deserved my acknowledgment of their year-long ruse. This was one of several rather embarrassing mistakes I made in learning that in that culture, it is impolite to disagree with or say "no" to a guest, and the principal and the dean of students had treated me as a guest in Al-Asnam.

The following fall, I was ready. After the first class had filed in on the first day of school and I had given them permission to be seated, the first thing I said was, "Who is 'le responsable de classe'?" A timid hand slowly went up. I asked the boy to stand. He stood. I asked to see the class's eraser. He showed it to me. I pointed at the corner of my desk nearest the door, and in a quite authoritative voice I said, "Every day when I come in the door, I want to see the eraser and four new pieces of chalk on that corner of the desk. If those items are not there, you will have four hours of detention. Do you understand?" The student said "Oui, Monsieur." I repeated that scene in each of my classes that day. And just as was the case the previous year, for this year also I had an eraser and chalk every day.

A couple days into that second year, some students clustered around my desk and asked where my sack was with the chalk and eraser. I laughed and said that this year I knew better, I did not have it any more. One smiled and said, "Oui, Monsieur, this year you know how to control the boys. C'est bien."

On occasion, I even entered into their system and helped them manage it. Every couple weeks as I was approaching the room for the next class, two or three students would intercept me and explain in hurried and excited voices, "The Thirds stole our eraser, and we know you'll be upset if you don't have the eraser, but it's not our fault. What shall we do?" I never figured out whether these "borrowed" erasers were real meanness or merely amusing tricks they played on each other. Either way, I responded, "That is not my problem. All I know is that when I come in the door, I need to see an eraser and chalk." Then I found important reasons to stop and confer with another teacher before I got to my room, giving my class plenty of time to "organize" for my coming appearance when I would enter the room and discover once again an eraser and chalk on my desk.

In Al-Asnam, our newly acquired appreciation for Catholicism was put to good use. There was a small Catholic congregation, staffed by two priests. In addition, a congregation of sisters operated a mother-child center. Mary's nursing work in Al-Asnam was with these sisters. One of her jobs was supporting women of families in a tent village, which had been erected after homes in a nearby village were washed away in a flood. When we showed up for mass on Sunday morning, we were welcomed warmly. They came to treat us like two of their parishioners, except that we did not receive communion. At one point, their comprehensive welcome surprised me. Cardinal Léon-Étienne Duval, whose Archbishopric of Algiers included Al-Asnam, made a yearly pastoral visit to the congregation. On a normal Sunday at mass, perhaps twenty people attended. For a mass with the cardinal, people came from farther out, and perhaps one hundred filled the small sanctuary. Cardinal Duval preached a good sermon on the biblical concept of love. At the close of the service, members of the audience were invited to join the cardinal in the living room of the priests' apartment for conversation and refreshments.

With an invitation to converse with a cardinal, I imagined that a large number of people would crowd into the priests' apartment. I asked one of the priests if it would be appropriate for us, who were not Catholics, to attend. "Mais oui," the priest said, "Of course you may come."

With some trepidation we entered the priests' small living room. Straight-back chairs were arranged in a circle. A table held plates of cheese and crackers, and a bottle of wine. Cardinal Duval was already seated. We picked up some refreshments and took seats. Others present were our two priests, some of the sisters, a few local parishioners, along with Mary and me—perhaps a dozen souls in all. There we were, somewhat awkwardly balancing our refreshments, and chatting with a cardinal. How so many folks, who had attended the earlier service, could pass up the opportunity to interact socially with a cardinal was a mystery to me.

At one point, I thanked the cardinal for his sermon on love, and I asked if this love went as far as refusing to bear arms in defense of self, country, or liberty. "Non," he said, "parce qu'il y a aussi la justice," that is, no, because there is also justice. After a bit more discussion, I indicated that I was a conscientious objector to war. "Vous avez le droit," the Cardinal Duval said, "le conseil l'a dit." I had the right to be a conscientious objector, he told me, because the council (Vatican II) had said it.

Only at this point did I explain that I was not a Catholic. At his inquiry, I explained that I was a Mennonite, a denomination descended from sixteenth-century Anabaptists. Although he appeared to know nothing of Mennonites or Anabaptists, he responded, "Quand même, je vois que vous avez une foi vive." Nonetheless, he said, I see that you have a live faith.

Russian support for Algeria included many technicians. Several families of Russian technicians lived in Al-Asnam and worked in the development of the Algerian oil industry. As a result of this support, when United States pundits of that era described the potential spread of the influence of the Communist Soviet Union, Algeria was often included as at least "leaning Communist." My own impression from the Algerians I knew in our village was that Algeria would accept aid from Russia but had no intention of becoming a Russian clone.

One Russian family lived in our stairwell, one floor above us. Others lived in adjacent stairwells of our building. Through contacts with these neighbors, we quickly learned that they were friendly people, quite different from the stereotype of dour, doctrinaire Russians popular in the United States ethos of that epoch. They were as curious about us as we were about them—each of us aware that we were their country's supposed adversary.

On occasion we shared meals with them. I played chess with a couple of the men, who could beat me soundly even when they were inebriated with vodka. Alexander, a tall blond only a few years older than I was, in particular sought me out. I played chess with Alexander. He offered to teach me some Russian in exchange for helping him to practice his English. Since the other Russians seemed to defer to Alexander, I assume that he was likely an intelligence officer, who kept track of his colleagues. It was a heady idea to think that Alexander may also have made a report on what the Americans in Al-Asnam were doing.

The Six-Day War in June 1967 produced a step forward in my learning about colonialism. I arrived in Algeria with an understanding of Israel and the Arab world about that found in Leon Uris' book *Exodus*, with its account of the heroic birth of a struggling nation amid more numerous enemies. As the war progressed, I listened to dramatically different news accounts on French and Algerian radio broadcasts.

Answers to questions I posed to some Algerian friends painted a markedly different picture than I received from *Exodus* or the standard American understanding of the status of Israel vis-à-vis Palestinians and the Arab nations. I heard about western powers, led by the United States, who without regard for the native population drew boundaries and created an alien entity populated by Europeans amid the Arab world. This creation occurred at the expense of the native Palestinian population, which was expected to cede its place to the newcomers.

When I cited the authority of the United Nations, my Algerian friends pointed to its recent creation and control by Europeans and rejected its authority to displace people who had lived in place for centuries. An Egyptian professor of Arabic in my lycée, who spoke English but not French, echoed the words of my Algerian friends. He told me that the creation of Israel was as if someone came in, killed my children, and took over my house, and that people from all over the world were doing this to the Arabs in Palestine.

In the long view, I came to see that Palestinians had a parallel experience and were forced into a similar status as that of First Nations peoples of North America in earlier centuries— forced off their ancestral lands by Europeans, with Palestinians living in refugee camps in Gaza, the West Bank, Jordan, and elsewhere, much as the First Nations peoples on reservations.

In short-term consideration, Russia supported the Arab cause in the Six-Day War, which earned the Russians a great deal of popularity with Algerians. Meanwhile, my wife and I were the only people from the United States living in our village of Al-Asnam. The United States was already unpopular because of the war in Vietnam, and now with this war we were citizens of the major power that supported Israel, which Algerians considered an enemy. When the war broke out, we had no idea what to expect, and we felt vulnerable.

Nonetheless, as I did every day, I walked through town to the lycêe Es-Salem to meet my classes. First thing, the *Proviseur* called me into his office. I had no idea what was coming, but his words were reassuring. He said that they knew that I was an upright person who could not be held responsible for what my government did. I should continue to come to school, he said, that I would be okay there, but that I should come directly to school and return home directly, and that it would be a good idea not to walk around outside at night. I thanked him warmly for his concern, support, and advice.

On the second night of the war, a pickup truck loaded with protestors pulled up in the parking lot outside the three-story building where we had a second-floor apartment. Chants began in French—"Da, Da Russe" and "A bas l'Amerique" and "L'Amerique à la poubel" (Yes, Yes, Russia; Down with America; America to the garbage can.)

To say the least, Mary and I were concerned. We quickly turned off our lights and lowered our shutters, and hoped we were invisible. We sat quietly inside, thinking about how to respond in a peaceful manner if we were approached.

We heard a knock on our door. I looked through the peephole. It was our Russian neighbors from the floor above us. I opened the door. "Come and stay with us tonight," they said. "If anyone comes to the door, we will talk to them."

We spent the night with these neighbors, dozing on their sofas. No one came to the door. The protestors left and never returned. Our Russian neighbors were good neighbors.

During the years that we lived in Algeria, quite apart from the Six-Day War, I listened to both French and Algerian news on the radio and I read French and Algerian newspapers. At the news shop in town I could buy *Le Monde*, the influential and internationally known French paper. In 1968, French president Charles de Gaulle was much in the news. As I recall, notable actions and policies of *le grand Charles*, as the 6-foot 5-inch de Gaulle was nicknamed, included these: vetoing British entry into the Common Market, refusing to sign a nuclear test ban treaty, expelling NATO headquarters from Paris, boycotting Israel after the Six-Day War, attacking the U.S. dollar as the standard for international currency, instituting university reforms that had students rioting in the streets of Paris for a month, and apparently supporting Quebec separatism.

This latter mention refers to a trip de Gaulle made to Canada, in which he bypassed the capital in Ottawa and went directly to Quebec where he gave a speech that concluded with the words, "Vive le Québec libre! Vive le Québec libre!" (Live free Quebec!). These actions perplexed and angered both French and American people. I certainly did not understand what de Gaulle was about. When I asked my French colleagues at school what de Gaulle was doing, the majority said, "C'est vieux est fou" (that old man is crazy) as they referred to the seventy-eight-year-old president. *Le Monde* even had an editorial with the headline "Est-il fou?" (Is he nuts?)

When I asked Jacques, my best French friend, what was going on with Charles de Gaulle, he had a different answer. It usually began "You have to understand," followed by a longish policy or history lesson. One day, probably weary of my questions, Jacques gave me a set of books and explained that everything I needed to know was in those three volumes. These books were a three-volume, profusely illustrated, gilt-edged, bound-in-embossed-leather, limited edition of de Gaulle's war memoir, his *Mémoires de Guerre*. Jacques's father was a Gaulist member of the French parliament. De Gaulle had prepared 600 copies of this special edition as gifts for his members in parliament. Jacques had his father's copy, and he loaned it to me.

De Gaulle's tomes proved to be fascinating reading. Written two decades earlier, the memoir read like a suspense novel. I spent several spellbound weeks reading about the experiences of *le grand Charles* in two world wars, as he led the forces of truth and justice, namely the French, against an array of opponents. The account was enlightening. Jacques was correct—what I needed to know was in these volumes. I learned that de

Gaulle believed that in World War II, the United States and Britain had failed to accord him the role and the respect that he thought he deserved. Thus he simply did not trust them. As I read his story, it became clear to me that his policies in 1968 were all designed to counter British and United States influence and to raise the profile of France at their expense. We might even say that he was getting even with Britain and the United States for their earlier attitudes. Rather than being the chaotic policies of a crazy old man, as most of my French colleagues said, the policies of 1968 reflected a coherent strategy, shaped by de Gaulle's experiences more than two decades earlier. One certainly did not have to agree with his actions, but the story brought clarity to them and would give insight to those who sought to counter the policies.

From this reading in de Gaulle's war memoirs, what I realized for the first time was how historical understanding can clarify issues in the present. In this particular case, a document written two decades earlier explained the current tumultuous context in France. After seeing how a bit of history clarified events in France, this insight about the potential impact of historical understanding caused me to question my intended career as a scholar and professor of the Old Testament and sparked a tentative change in anticipated career direction. In fact, I did eventually decide that the way to understand and influence the contemporary church was through an understanding of its history. Without this reading of the memoir of *le grand Charles*, I would have had a very different career. His *Mémoires de Guerre* became the first of the three literary works described in this memoir that changed the direction of my career.

The two years we spent in Algeria produced learnings and had an impact on my life beyond any brief description. Teaching in the lycée took a lot of mental energy, and I never fully relaxed in the job. I was handed a textbook for each level, and beyond that I was on my own to figure out how and what to teach. The first year was a struggle as I dealt with order in class as well as learning how the system worked. The second year went better. If I had stayed for a third year, I think I would have been a reasonably effective teacher. I regret that the energy that went into my teaching did not allow for more interaction with Algerian people beyond the lycée.

We did have Algerian friends. One was a couple that I will call Mr. and Mrs. Mohammed. He taught physical education, and she was the principal of the girl's side of the lycée. They had attended university, and she was one of the few Muslim women in our town who did not wear a veil. I gathered that they moved from Algiers to Al-Asnam to be less visible after Mr. Mohammed's previous engagement in radical political activity. Once when a girl in my class broke into tears for no reason that I perceived, I went to Mrs. Mohammed and reported that the student perhaps had a problem that should be checked on. I learned later that the principal was impressed—no French teacher had ever expressed that kind of concern about a student, which indicated something of the educational milieu.

There was a small tennis club in Al-Asnam, where I paid $20 per year for a membership. Both Algerians and French teachers played there. I played with anyone who was around, but most often I played with M. Sayiah, an Algerian man much older than I. He usually beat me by being very steady and keeping the ball in play until I missed. On one occasion, I was asked why I played with the Algerians but the French people never did. I was embarrassed that I had not noticed. After that, I made a point of playing with Algerians, and rarely joined the French players, who clearly kept to themselves.

Through speaking French in class every day, along with my interactions with other teachers and friends in all manner of contexts, I developed an easy facility with French. I read novels for pleasure. Although it has been many years since I last read it, I still list Victor Hugo's *Les Misérables*, with its theme of forgiveness, as my all-time favorite novel. I enjoyed functioning in a new language. I relished the sense of being a different person, standing outside myself, watching and wondering who this man was that was speaking French with these people.

Living in an Algerian village had its challenges but was also intensely interesting. It was summer when we arrived. I assumed that I could be efficient and ignore the temperature. I walked outside to do our grocery shopping. Stepping into the heat was like walking into a hot blanket. However, I kept going for the half-mile walk to town. Although few people were out, the shops were open, with the owners reclining in the back. They did serve me with my purchases. I made it home—and I took a nap. It became more than obvious why things closed down for a nap during the hot part of the day, and that I needed to learn the ways of this culture.

I came to enjoy frequent grocery shopping on Rue D'Isly, the main street of Al-Asnam. I carried a *filet*, a woven net that expanded as purchases were added to it. I made stops at a vegetable shop, a fruit stand, a meat market, a store for packaged goods, and more. Three items still spark fond memories. For one, we could purchase oranges picked fresh from nearby orchards—the most flavorful oranges we ever ate.

The second item I found in the seafood market. The vender had a tub full of small squid, perhaps six to eight inches long. I asked about preparation. He showed me a simple cleaning process—two knife cuts to remove the beak and the ink sac, strip out the intestines and the internal skeleton, and then cut the body and tentacles into small pieces for cooking. After that, I picked up squid on a regular basis and took them home where Mary fried them.

The third item was ripe dates, which I had always liked. In the shop in Al-Asnam, I was delighted to find ripe dates still attached to the branch. I ate a lot of them. One day, on a whim I cut the date open with a knife and extracted the seed before popping it into my mouth—and I discovered that the date contained a small white worm. I flicked it away before eating the date. I cut open another date, and found another worm. After exploring several more, I concluded that most dates had a worm inside, which meant that I had eaten a lot of worms. Despite the potential for the extra protein the worms provided, after that experience, I always cut dates open before eating.

In addition to learning about the issue of justice for Palestinians, living in Algeria was the beginning of my learning that there is an Arab, Muslim world. In Al-Asnam and Algiers, we experienced a small sample of one corner of this world. The call to prayer five times per day became routine and expected sounds.

Twice we watched friends and neighbors practice fasting during the month of Ramadan. The school day was shortened, since the lunch period was eliminated. Since students had been up late to eat after fasting all day and then rose early to eat breakfast before sun up, they came to school tired and classes were more calm than usual.

I began to learn that the Quran, the Muslim holy book, had a number of prophets that were found in the Christian Bible, including Jesus. It was the beginning of my awareness that Muslims had a centuries-long awareness of Christianity, and it was not particularly positive. Christianity was the religion that for centuries had launched crusades against Muslims.

My experience with the chalk, with the culture that does not say "no" to a guest, and much more, made me wonder how much political animosity begins with a simple misreading of the other. When we left Algeria after two years, I had the beginning of awareness of the necessity of being slow to assume that I had understood someone speaking another language or reflecting a different culture. Although I would not miss teaching English in a lycée, I did have a bit of regret about not spending a third year when I might have been a real teacher in that system. I would genuinely miss the experience of living in an Arab culture and exercising my French language skills every day. On the other hand, I was eager for the next stage in my journey to become a professor and eager to begin learning German.

From Algeria, we went to Germany, where we lived from summer 1968 to summer 1969. I knew that graduate schools in religion usually required knowledge of two foreign languages. I had French well in hand. The principal goal of this year was to learn as much German as possible. We spent a two-month term studying German at a Goethe Institute in Iserlohn. From there, I enrolled in Kirchliche Hochschule Bethel at Bethel bei Beilefield, a school recommended to me by AMBS professor Clarence Bauman. The Kirchliche Hochschule was a part of the German university system that taught Bible, church history, and theology.

At the Hochschule, I enrolled in a seminar to review biblical Hebrew, and I heard lectures on church history. I wrote several term papers in German and used every opportunity to speak German. In one year, I did not attain the level of familiarity in German that I achieved in French after three years. However, I developed conversational and reading knowledge of German. In my later career, the year in Germany more than fulfilled its purpose through writing I did using historic Anabaptist and Mennonite sources in German.

In summer of 1969, we returned to the United States. In the four years abroad, I had learned much about the world. I was much more aware of the presence of injustice in the world, particularly that related to colonialism, which sensitized me to the racism in United States history and in theology. I had learned of the injustice perpetrated on Palestinians with support from the United States. I was fully aware of and opposed to the war in Vietnam. Sometimes when I was asked what I was, wryly I would explain that I wanted to say Mennonite rather than American.

I had acquired working knowledge of two languages in addition to English, and I greatly enjoyed learning to make my way in a different culture while using a language other than English. Even with the allure of a future in graduate school, I was not looking forward to returning to the United States and its problematic politics. In terms of some of my previous views, I had moved beyond nonresistance and now advocated nonviolent activism. I had learned that Catholics were Christians in a more fulsome way. After reading the *Mémoires de Guerre* by Charles de Gaulle, I was well on the way to switching my intended graduate school focus from Old Testament to church history.

7

Charles de Gaulle Realized

After four years abroad, I enrolled for a final year at Associated Mennonite Biblical Seminaries, now fully in Elkhart, Indiana, with Goshen Biblical Seminary having completed its move from Goshen. I lived in nearby Goshen and commuted to school with several other students. It would be a momentous year, both academically and personally.

I enrolled in a full load of courses, continuing to study Hebrew language and taking another course in the prophets. I was thrilled when Millard Lind invited me to be the student assistant to the Bible Department. Meanwhile, I also took church history and a course in Anabaptist history. The obvious question I contemplated was which direction I would pursue in my anticipated graduate school career.

In Anabaptist history, I posed what I considered a loaded question, namely this: How was it that the sixteenth-century Anabaptists and modern Mennonites both knew how to make the Bible come out right on rejection of the sword, although the technique we learned in our biblical exegesis class at AMBS was different from that of the early Anabaptists?

The professor, J. C. Wenger, was now my father-in-law. The question had a definite edge but was real, and I pushed ahead. He seemed taken aback by the challenge but said something on the order of presuppositions that we bring to any methodology. It was my first time to hear that idea. At the time, I was not impressed. But from the perspective of my later learning, I understand what he meant, and I recognize how assumptions and values we bring impact the application of a particular methodology. In Anabaptist perspective, these values come from the narrative of Jesus. Some years later, I had occasion to ask Wenger whether he remembered the question or his answer. He did not, but I told him that it was a better answer than I recognized at the time.

I also took a course on the church and race, in which I read James Cone's *Black Theology and Black Power*. With the heightened sensitivity to racism that I had gained from living in Algeria where I saw the impact of European, colonial domination, Cone's unflinching indictment of American racism was sobering. In the naïveté with which I read the book, it was also frightening. Cone wrote that Jesus was black and that black was the color of opposition to racism. To oppose racism, one had to be black.

As I read through the book, I acknowledged the truth of his argument while questioning whether there was hope for me as white. Finally in the conclusion, I read where Cone said that black was a symbol and that white people could be black if they joined the struggle against racism. I heaved a big metaphorical sigh—there was hope for me.

Twenty years later, *Black Theology and Black Power* returned with a different kind of contribution to my learning. When I reread the book I started with the introduction. There, at the beginning of the book I read that white people who joined the struggle against racism could be black. In the intervening years I had learned a seemingly obvious fact, namely that an introduction to a book served a real purpose! Meanwhile, at that point, the book assisted me in another way, as a following chapter recounts.

On two occasions, I acted on my recently acquired belief in active nonviolence. The seminaries canceled classes for a day, and held a teach-in about the war in Vietnam. The events of the day were posted, with presentations and discussions in morning and afternoon, culminating with a public activity in downtown Elkhart, where we would pass out antiwar leaflets. The events of the teach-in took place in the reading room of the library, adjacent to the stacks. I was recently returned from Algeria and then Germany. In my four years abroad, I had encountered plenty of opinion against American policy and this war and was still experiencing the cultural shock of returning to the country that prosecuted the war. I was in no mood to spend a day hearing presentations on material I was already well aware of and otherwise let the seminary know the obvious, namely that I opposed the war. I spent the day in the upper stacks, a half-flight of stairs above the reading room, attempting to work on a term paper.

At the end of the day, I joined the teach-in for the activity downtown, which I considered the most important event of the day. It was the public action that would move beyond "preaching to the choir," that is, presentations at a seminary of the peace church to students who supposedly were already convinced of the truth of Jesus' rejection of the sword, and engage in an activity that would speak to the wider world. For this public activity, the seminary students joined with a larger effort in the city. I was assigned to distribute leaflets in an affluent area of the city.

Elkhart is located in a conservative area and state. Most of the people I contacted that day told me that President Nixon knew more about the war than those of us who protested, and we had no right to challenge him. On my side, I was surprised that only a dozen seminary students participated in what I had considered the most important event of the day.

Another day, in conjunction with a national march against the war in Washington, an invitation was posted for seminary students to undertake a protest at the nearby Pierre Moran mall. I accompanied other seminary students, as we walked a couple hundred yards from the seminary across an expanse of grass and into the mall. We took places outside a grocery store and held signs that protested the war in Vietnam. This time only two students in addition to myself participated in the nonviolent public activity. Participating in these public acts gave me a sense of inner cleansing, as though for a brief moment I was ridding myself of my nation's corrupt war, but I had not realized that I was ahead of most Mennonites in moving to the stance of nonviolent activism.

An activity during orientation days of the year raised a different kind of question about nonviolence. Outside resource persons from a counseling organization I no longer recall led us in a group activity. To begin, the leader told us to sit on the floor, with our eyes lowered, not looking at anyone else. After a bit, we were told to stand, still without looking at anyone. Next, with eyes still down, to begin walking slowly in a circle. Then, to walk a bit faster. Next we were to lift our eyes and look at the others. The next command was to walk a bit faster and to bump someone. Then speed up and bump someone a little harder.

By that time, I was anticipating the next command and I was eager to bump someone vigorously—and the leader halted the exercise. "Do you know what was happening?" the leader said. "You men have a lot of suppressed aggression. In another minute, you would have been fighting each other." Some older faculty were offended. I overheard one say that the leader's statement was not true because "we have victory in Christ over aggression."

For myself, I recognized the truth of what the leader had said about aggression. It influenced the way some years later I came to see that competitive athletics is compatible with a commitment to nonviolence. For those so inclined, competitive athletics is an appropriate way to express aggression. When individuals or teams compete within the rules and with respect for their opponents, each is pushing the other to play better and to improve their game. That is, the individuals and teams actually help each other to improve, and within a sense of mutual benefit and respect, a competitive sport can actually be a cooperative activity.

An incident from the church and ministry class produced another challenge to an inherited idea. Small groups of maybe six students from the class met in extended sessions. My group met from 2:30 to 10 pm. During this time, every word spoken had to be said to the entire group. If anyone left for a restroom break, silence would ensue until the person returned. For supper, a bucket of Kentucky Fried Chicken was brought in, with enough pieces for each of us to have two. I prefer dark meat, but the first time the bucket came by I passed up a drumstick and took a piece of white meat that I considered less desirable. The second time around, however, a drumstick remained—I decided to be self-serving and took the piece that I wanted.

Later, on a whim, I polled the group about their preferences of white or dark meat, and then how they approached the choice when the bucket was passed. It turned out that the class was evenly divided between preference for white or dark meat and also that each of us had made the same choice that I had—deferring to others by taking a less preferred piece the first time around but acting on what felt like a self-serving motive the next time and taking the piece that we preferred.

It was striking—without any prior discussion about preferences, we had each acted on the same impulses of first deferring our preference and then acting on what felt like self-interest the second time. Each of us could have had two of our favorite pieces if we had exercised what felt like self-interest both times.

Later I would learn that books on Mennonite history describe the "humility tradition" that was strong in the nineteenth century and began to fade for progressive Mennonites in the twentieth century. In this tradition, acts of self-interest, self-promotion, and self-aggrandizement were strongly discouraged; deferring to others and to the wishes of the community was encouraged. For example, I recall my father saying that when playing a game I should be glad that I lost so that the others could have fun too. This incident with the choice of chicken pieces appeared to display the remnants of this humility tradition, even among outwardly acculturated and progressive Mennonite seminary students in 1970.

In addition to course work, the important task of the fall was to make a decision about graduate school. I had taken courses that renewed my interest in the Old Testament. But the impulse toward church history sparked by the reading of Charles de Gaulle's *Mémoires de Guerre*.remained dominant. I liked the idea of being immersed in the ongoing stream of the history of the church. I discussed the possibilities with a number of professors before finalizing the decision. Since I had done a lot of work with Millard Lind and had worked as the assistant to the Bible Department, he expressed some surprise—and then pledged support—when I informed him that I had opted for graduate work in church history. That fall, I applied to graduate schools where I could focus on church history.

In that era, Anabaptism still reigned as the popular "in" topic in seminary. It was commonly assumed that there was, or ought to be, an Anabaptist perspective on anything, even basket weaving, as the joke would go. In fact, some years later, in his humorous account of the newly appearing category of Mennonite Urban Professionals, namely Muppies, Emerson Lesher would write in *The Muppie Manual* that the intellectual Muppie was busy writing an article or book on "Anabaptism/Mennonites and something." In this milieu of 1969, when I decided to study church history, engaging in Anabaptist history seemed virtually a given.

I controlled the decision about an area of study in graduate school. Gaining admission to graduate school involved elements beyond my control. After having anticipated this point for six years, I was tense. Not being admitted loomed as a genuinely fearsome thought. After several applications, I had three options. Mary was visiting at her parents' house a half block from our upstairs apartment, when I got home from school and found the envelope from Duke University. With trembling hands I tore it open. Waving the acceptance letter, I ran down the block to show Mary and her parents,

8

Anabaptist Scholar

In the fall of 1970 we moved to Durham, North Carolina, and I enrolled at Duke University in the PhD program in religion jointly administered by the graduate school of the university and the Duke Divinity school. We spent four years in Durham. It was an exciting and intimidating new world.

The Duke University west campus was constructed as a unit in the 1920s. A drive enters the center of the campus, with wings stretching to each side. At the top of the drive is the tall chapel, which unknowing visitors called a cathedral. This entire campus is constructed in Gothic style, giving the campus a venerable and majestic air. The divinity school where I attended classes was in the building immediately to the right as one approached the chapel. Every day that I walked there I remained in awe of the surroundings.

My major professor was David Steinmetz. Dr. Steinmetz stood an inch or so over six feet, a round face with full cheeks atop a full torso. He had a calm, resonant baritone voice, but when the occasion demanded he spoke with authority. I picture him in brown suits—a gentle bear.

Dr. Steinmetz was a specialist in the Reformation but above all in Martin Luther. I sat in on his lectures to a divinity dchool class on the history of the Reformation. I was introduced to the story of Martin Luther's progress to the Diet of Worms: beginning university in the study of law; precipitous entry to the monastery; education in nominalist theology and his search for a gracious God; earning a doctor of theology degree and becom-

77

ing professor of Bible at the University of Wittenberg; discovery of "justification by faith;" the 95 *Theses* that protested indulgences; the indulgence controversy; the under-the-table deal between Bishop Albert of Brandenburg, Pope Leo X, and banker Jacob Fugger that enabled the sale of the indulgence Luther protested; *Exsurge Domine*, the papal bull that excommunicated Luther in 1520; his lonely and heroic declaration of "Here I stand" at .the Diet of Worms in 1521, followed by Emperor Charles V's declaration making Luther an outlaw of the empire.

I did a number of seminars with Dr. Steinmetz. Between *Exsurge Domine* and the Diet of Worms, Luther wrote the three tracts that contained the heart of his new, reformed theology. In a seminar on Luther, I read the 95 *Theses*, which precipitated the Reformation, and the three important tracts: *Freedom of the Christian*, which presented Luther's idea of justification by faith; *The Babylonian Captivity of the Church* that explained Luther's view of the eucharist, in which he rejected Catholicism's idea that the bread and wine at communion turned into the body and blood of Jesus (called transubstantiation) but retained the idea of a real presence of the body of Christ in the bread and wine; and finally, Luther's *Address to the Nobility of the German Nation* put forward the idea of the universal priesthood of all believers, which authorized the secular rulers to exercise this priesthood by carrying out church reform when the Roman clergy refused to do so. We also read Luther's ferocious condemnation of rebellious peasants and of Anabaptists.

The Martin Luther who precipitated the Protestant Reformation became a larger than life figure for me. Later as a professor, I always enjoyed rehearsing his journey to reformation, following the story I learned from Dr. Steinmetz, including some of his favorite jokes about Luther, such as the comment that the sayings recorded in Luther's "Table Talk" came when he was "full of beer and sausage." Even as I came to recognize his flaws, Luther personified the Reformation for me, and any discussion of Anabaptist origins needed to start with a mention of Luther's challenge to the church in Rome.

In a seminar on John Calvin, we read the two big volumes of Calvin's systematic theology, his *Institutes of the Christian Reli-*

gion. It is well known that John Calvin believed in predestination, but I learned that Calvin, like Martin Luther, did not make it a doctrine about God. Rather, it was about salvation. Both Luther and Calvin came to believe in predestination when they discovered that they believed even though they could do nothing to save themselves. It was later Calvinists who made predestination a doctrine about the nature of God. In another seminar, we read *Spiritual and Anabaptist Writers* and other Anabaptist literature. My papers for this seminar were my first systematic interaction with historic Anabaptist writings.

Studying writings of John Calvin presented me with what now seems a commonplace. Calvin's story may have been part of the Reformation, but his theology had an identifiable trajectory that differed from that of Martin Luther, and further, a wide variety of beliefs came under the umbrella of "Protestant." That simple insight sat quietly but eventually contributed to my conviction that Anabaptists and Mennonite could and should also develop theology that reflected their tradition.

A final seminar was in Catholic Reformation and Counter Reformation. One resource was the *Spiritual Exercises* of Ignatius of Loyola, who founded the Jesuits as an order whose purpose became responding to the Protestant Reformation. A minor but striking point in the *Exercises* was one of his rules for thinking with the church, namely to believe that the white one sees is black if the hierarchical church says so.

Other reading included documents from the Council of Trent, whose response to Protestantism defined the Catholic Church until the middle of the twentieth century. It was the work of Trent that the council Vatican II reformed, whose impact we benefited from during our French study in Brussels and then in Algeria. I valued this seminar greatly, for expanding my understanding of Catholicism and for emphasizing the obvious point that church history was not limited to the story of Protestantism.

Dr. Steinmetz guided my dissertation on views of the Holy Spirit in Anabaptist theology. This dissertation was never published, but it exposed me to techniques of analysis as well as a great deal of literature that served me well in future years. I waited outside the room after my dissertation defense. Dr. Steinmetz came out and extended his hand. He said, "You passed. You are a doctor now. My name is David." I shook his hand gratefully.

Given my relatively recent decision to switch from Old Testament to church history for graduate study, I wondered if my background was weak. In any case, when I arrived at Duke University, I was not a confident student. David supported me, and I responded well to his guidance. He gave me a thorough grounding in Reformation theologies. Some years later, that foundation was validated when he asked me to write the article on "Pacifism" for the *Oxford Encyclopedia of the Reformation*, for which he was an assistant editor.

David's influence went beyond what I learned about the Reformation of the sixteenth century. He gave me my first lesson in learning to write. Back in seminary when I was still considering study of Old Testament, Millard Lind advised me to focus on Hebrew language, saying that there would be plenty of time for writing in graduate school. However, I could have used some advice on writing.

In my first semester with David, I ventured into his office to pick up a term paper. He indicated that I should check one of the internal pages. I did. On it were some thirteen red circles. On that page, he had circled all the passive constructions and appearances of some form of the verb "to be."

I looked at David. "Denny," he said, "there are more verbs in the English language than 'to be.' If you want to write a dissertation with me, you will need to learn to use some of those verbs."

I could only recognize the truth of the critique. In future writing, I began circling occurrences of "to be" and passive constructions and paid particular attention to keeping their number as low as possible.

Some years later as a professor, when I had my own classes and I had learned enough to sound credible when I talked about writing, I developed a list of "Top Ten Writing Errors that Annoy Professor Weaver," in which avoiding passives appeared as a prominent item. I distributed this list to all classes and told them that I did not want to hear their pages buzzing like a hive of bees.

When I talked about that item with my students, I was channeling David Steinmetz.

Beyond the Reformation, I was introduced to additional material that would prove valuable in coming years. For one, I drove the few miles to Chapel Hill to take a course in the Renaissance with John Headley at the University of North Carolina. The Renaissance impulse of "back to the sources" applied to the reformers and in particular Anabaptists, who returned to the Bible. Reformers used the biblical text to critique papal declarations.

I had a minor in American religion with Professor Stuart Henry, whom I learned to know rather well. Professor Henry was of average build, a bachelor who lived alone. What distinguished him was his choice of dress. He wore nothing but a black suit with white shirt and black tie. As he explained, dressing in this black uniform made his life much simpler. He never had to go shopping. He could merely telephone the clothing store and order black suits and white shirts in his size, and when he got dressed in the morning, the decision about what to wear for the day was already made as well.

From Professor Henry I learned about the first Puritan settlers in New England, who through a chain of events in Europe, had acquired Calvinist theology. Although Puritans are not today's Evangelicals, today's Evangelicals descended from the Puritans who espoused Calvinism. Luther may have been my sometime hero, but this link of Evangelicalism to John Calvin makes him the most widely influential figure of the Protestant Reformation.

Not only do a number of denominations in the United States have roots in Calvinism, in a series of developments unnecessary to detail here, the Puritan vision of being a "new Israel" escaping from an evil Europe with God's help to become a "city on the hill" became the foundation for the United States' claim to be a "Christian nation." Other transformations of the Puritan vision include the nineteenth-century slogan of Manifest Destiny, today's civil religion, and the claim of "American exceptionalism." Professor Henry introduced us to the role of racism in United States denominations.

This broad knowledge of American religion became valuable in my later efforts to write theology for Mennonites in the American context, a theology that would pose a challenge to the several varieties of national ideology that claim ultimate allegiance, as well as data on the foundation of the nation built on stolen land and stolen labor that would stimulate my attraction to Black theology.

Much earlier, I had naively assumed that getting into graduate school was the big worry to face when considering a career as a professor of religion. No sooner did I arrive in graduate school than I learned about and started facing the problem of finding a teaching job. That worry sat in the back of my mind the entire time I was at Duke. Thus receiving an offer to move to Goshen College for a two-year assignment while Norman Kraus was on leave, offered a sense of relief. Mary and I made the move.

TWO

OPENING MOVES

9

A Beginning

In fall of 1974, I arrived at Goshen College as a replacement for Norman Kraus, who was on a two-year leave. Offices for religion and Bible faculty lined the corridor in what had previously been the Goshen Seminary building. Moving into an office in the lineup once inhabited by my former, highly respected seminary professors was inspiring as well as a bit intimidating. It took a while to live into the role of "Professor."

A particular highlight of the year was the visit to Goshen College of Yale church historian Roland Bainton. As he sat in a meeting with religion faculty, he sketched images of the people sitting around him. Tucked away in a file of mementos, I have preserved two drawings of myself signed by Roland H. Bainton.

Fresh from Duke University where I had studied Reformation history and thought, I considered myself a Reformation scholar, and I had designs on writing some kind of major work on sixteenth-century Anabaptist theology. Thus the appearance of "Christian Faith" on the list of courses I was expected to teach did not excite me. In fact, it intimidated me. The course was an introduction to Christian theology for college students. Since I had studied Reformation era history and thought at Duke, my experience with theology was limited to the course "Preface to Theology," which I had taken at Associated Mennonite Biblical Seminaries five years earlier from influential Mennonite theologian John Howard Yoder.

Other than knowing that the course should explain the central doctrines of Christology, Trinity, and atonement, I had little

idea what to deal with nor how to go about it in a course called
"Christian Faith." Neither did I have any idea how this course
would eventually shape my career.

As I prepared for Christian Faith, I had a question for my
colleagues Stanley Shenk and J. Richard Burkholder: "Is there a
Mennonite perspective on these issues?" Their answer surprised
me. In this era, the interest remained strong in the Anabaptism
that sparked my particular graduate school focus. Frequently
the question arose about an Anabaptist perspective on just
about any subject. Thus when I asked about an Anabaptist or
Mennonite perspective on theology, I expected to receive a re-
ferral to several articles or a book that would guide me. Instead,
the question produced shrugs and statements of "I don't know."

I began the course Christian Faith with that question in the
back of my mind but with no idea that I would spend my career
answering it. When I did start to answer the question, I assumed
that producing a theology that reflected an Anabaptist perspective would be welcomed by Mennonites. The resistance that
emerged, and continued throughout my career, surprised me.

Meanwhile, that first semester was a struggle for me as well
as for the students, an inauspicious start for a course that I
would teach under several names some forty-six times throughout my career. In later years, if I encountered a student from that
first class, my inclination was to apologize.

One bright spot did emerge from that class—a first indica-
tion of the direction which my eventual theologizing would take.
I had used Gustav Aulén's classic statement *Christus Victor* to
sketch the three historic atonement formulas. Toward the end of
that first semester, a student whose name has faded into the
mists of time asked what was going on with these formulas. On
impulse I threw out the idea that the atonement images reflected
different understandings of the church. Thus first surfaced in
embryonic form the idea that I would develop in articles and
books over much of my career.

In early summer I received a surprise, a phone call from
Elmer Neufeld, dean at Bluffton College, offering me the oppor-
tunity to join the Religion Department of Bluffton College.
Theeattraction was the possibility of an open-ended position.

On the other hand, as a graduate of Goshen and identified with Goshen's denomination of Mennonites, staying in Goshen was attractive. After discussion with Mary and with Goshen's dean, we decided to make the move. In mid-summer of 1975, I moved with my family to Bluffton College, now University, in Bluffton, Ohio, for a potentially long-term position. It would be a number of years before I realized how fortunate I was to be at Bluffton. Meanwhile, in this new position, I continued to teach an introductory course in Christian theology.

Early in my preparation for the theology course, I pulled out my five-year-old-notes from Yoder's "Preface to Theology." (Chapter 23 to follow recounts my later learning about and dealing with John Howard Yoder's abusive conduct toward women.) The first time through they served merely as my source to the standard or "orthodox" formulas of Christology from the councils of Nicea (325 CE) and Chalcedon (451 CE) and the doctrine of the Trinity from the three Cappadocian Fathers. Nicea defined Jesus as "one substance with the Father" or "one in being with the Father" in a creed that was lightly revised by the Council of Constantinople in 381 CE, and in this form is still repeated today. Chalcedon produced the formula that identified Jesus as "truly human and truly God." The three Cappadocians—Basil of Caesarea (330-379 CE), his younger brother Gregory of Nyssa (335-395 CE), and Gregory of Nazianzus (329-389 CE)—developed the trinitarian terminology of "one God in three Persons."

I was relieved when I learned that AMBS had made a transcription of Yoder's class lectures. I obtained this printed version of *Preface to Theology*, which became my primary source for Christology and Trinity in my theology class. As I used *Preface*, it soon became clear that Yoder was not merely endorsing the standard or "orthodox" statements of Christology and Trinity. Rather, the lectures relativized these statements—showing that they were written by men to answer specific questions and reflected the particular context and worldview in which they emerged.

This insight opened the door, I realized, for us in the twentieth century who inhabit a different context and worldview to develop additional ways to talk about the same issues without being beholden to the inherited, creedal language. In other words, the classic statements were not unquestioned givens to be taught and repeated. They were particular statements, and there could be other ways to answer the same questions. Of course, these issues are much clearer to me now than they were early in my career, and I was as yet unaware how intense the pushback would be when I published these relativizing ideas.

Preface to Theology opened my mind to the fact that all theology, even the classic statements of Christology and Trinity that enjoyed the status of supposed transcendent, unquestioned givens, is always relative to a context and subject to revision and restatement. This insight stimulated my ongoing question of whether there was a specifically Mennonite—later peace church or nonviolent—way to discuss the classic questions. Without *Preface* I may well have taught the theology class as a routine summary of tradition, and I would have spent more of my time dealing with early Anabaptist theology.

Instead *Preface* set me on a trajectory that would eventually find me well beyond Yoder's views and using theologies he never addressed. That led fifteen years later to the publication of my major book on nonviolent atonement and following that a book on nonviolent God. Because of this shaping impulse and trajectory on which it set me, after Charles de Gaulle's *Mémoires de Guerre*, John Howard Yoder's *Preface to Theology* became the second of three books that materially changed the direction of my career as professor and theologian.

In the immediate context of my realization that Yoder had opened the door to alternatives to the classic formulas, my question about a "Mennonite perspective" on theology returned, this time in terms of a believers church perspective. Is there a specifically believers church Christology, I wondered?

Believers church is not the opposite of a church of unbelievers. The term emerged after 1955 to describe the sixteenth-century Radical Reformation groups that rejected baptism of infants, the rite of entry into the church that encompassed the mass of society. Those who resisted baptism of infants insisted that the church consisted of people who had made an adult decision to be baptized—thus adult believers and a believers church.

In the twenty-first century, in which in many settings there is no church of the masses and no established church, and every church consists of people who made a voluntary decision to belong, believers church is still used to designate a church that is distinct from society and that does not expect civil government to enforce its policies. The believers church concept includes Mennonites, Church of the Brethren, Quakers, elements of the Catholic Church, some African-American denominations, and elements of other groups.

In 1967, a large and carefully planned conference involving leading scholars, denominational executives, and pastors met at Southern Baptist Theological Seminary in Louisville, Kentucky, to study and clarify the concept of the believers church. The results received wide publicity in denominational periodicals.

Interest from this conference led to the loosely organized Committee on Continuing Conversations on the Concept of the Believers Church, which gave guidance to denominations or institutions that wished to sponsor a conference. John Howard Yoder and Church of the Brethren historian Donald Durnbaugh served as co-chairs of this committee.

Thus early in 1980, after securing permission from Bluffton president Elmer Neufeld, I contacted Durnbaugh and Yoder and arranged with them to organize a conference at Bluffton College on the question of whether there is a Christology that specifically reflects the believers church. I made phone calls and put together a representative committee that met in Fort Wayne, Indiana, to develop a program. Present were Donald Durnbaugh and Ken Brown from the Church of the Brethren, Quaker Wilmer Cooper, and Mennonites Norman Kraus, John Howard Yoder, Elmer Neufeld, and myself.

We outlined the issues for the program, with the planners at Bluffton left to identify the people to fill each program slot. The eventual program had a series of impressive speakers that included representatives from a variety of believers church perspectives, both Catholic and various Protestant denominations.

The conference itself met on parts of three days in October 1980, with John Howard Yoder as keynote speaker. Yoder's keynote address presented four New Testament images of

Christology, later expanded to five in the published version. Although no one recognized it at the time, Yoder was showing the way for the contemporary believers church to develop approaches to Christology that could bypass the formulas of Nicea and Chalcedon and make sense in the twentieth century.

As the conference rolled along, I realized that none of the conference speakers spoke directly to the question of whether there was or could be a specifically believers church Christology. As a still young professor, however, I lacked the courage to challenge the well-known, senior speakers that we had engaged.

Yoder made available a post-conference edition of his keynote address with an addendum. Here he congratulated the conference planners for going beyond clarifying the believers church concept, as previous conferences had done, in an effort to apply the concept to another question. He listed developments that made the conference important, one of which was his "relativizing" of the standard christological categories from Nicea and Chalcedon in his *Preface* lectures. He also wrote that conference planners had been awed by the big names on the program and none had challenged speakers to answer the conference question. Since I had originated the idea of the conference, it certainly felt like that comment addressed my timidity.

In later years I have often wished that I could replay that conference. With the help of a major revision from Yoder, I did publish an article in the April 1983 *Mennonite Quarterly Review* that summarized the conference presentations and pointed to implications for a believers church Christology. I also take a bit of consolation from a later comment by Brethren scholar Dale Brown, who told me that because of this conference, he credited me with the beginning of the conversation about a specific believers church theology.

Meanwhile, the task that took the majority of my time was teaching. I cycled through courses in "Protestant Christianity"; "American Religion"; and "War, Peace, and Nonviolence." But the course that was starting to occupy my interest was the course in Christian theology. With it, I was continuing to fill out my understanding of Christology and also developing a particular, believers church perspective on atonement.

I still defined myself as a sixteenth-century Anabaptist and Reformation scholar, but my dabbling in theology became increasingly attractive. Given the frequent question about the Anabaptist perspective on something or anything, I assumed that producing a theology that reflected an Anabaptist perspective would be warmly welcomed. I was soon to be disabused of that assumption.

10

The Last Word

Dutch immigrant Ted VanderEnde graduated from the well-known fundamentalist institution Dallas Theological Seminary and in 1984 was pastor at St. John Mennonite church in Pandora, eight miles from Bluffton where I lived and taught at Bluffton College. Clad in dark blue suit with accompanying conservative tie, broad-shouldered, wavy, jet black hair over wide face, speaking in fluent but accented English, VanderEnde stood at the podium and portrayed me as the epitome of all that was wrong with Mennonite higher education—rejection of authority of the Bible by accepting destructive higher criticism, refusing to believe in absolutes, and advocating a process theology.

I was sitting in the fourth row of a meeting room packed with perhaps one hundred people. I was still new to the discipline of theology and the attack blindsided me. I was numb, and a bit scared—could this impact my status at Bluffton College, where the president kept pushing an Evangelical outlook?

The occasion was an October 1984 conference, meeting in a retreat center at Camp Wonderland at Camp Lake, Wisconsin. The conference was called to deal with the recent Smoketown controversy. A group of Evangelical and Fundamentalist pastors had met at the Smoketown Mennonite Church in Pennsylvania and produced a statement that accused prominent professors at Associated Mennonite Biblical Seminaries (AMBS) and some colleges of destroying the Bible by teaching the Documentary Hypothesis of the Pentateuch, accepting evolution rather than pushing six-day creation on the basis of Genesis, teaching that Jonah was a myth about the history of Israel, and more.

The pastors' statement had put on evident display that the Mennonite Church and the General Conference Mennonite Church, the two largest North American Mennonite denominations of that era (now merged), still harbored a contemporary version of the modernist-fundamentalist controversy that arose in the late nineteenth and early twentieth centuries. This eruption in the 1980s appeared to catch church leaders by surprise. I recall a statement from C. J. Dyck, venerable professor of church history at AMBS, that "We thought that the modernist-fundamentalist controversy was behind us." The stated purpose of the conference at Camp Wonderland was for the two sides to engage in dialogue, while the implicit agenda of the gathering was to reassure conservatives that there was still a place for them even as the churches evolved in a progressive direction.

At this point in the first third of my teaching career, I still considered myself a Reformation historian. I had started working on the project that would become my first book, a popular history of sixteenth-century Anabaptism based on recent scholarship. I had recently published an article in *The Mennonite*, the publication of the General Conference Mennonite Church, in which I argued that recent changes in our understanding of Anabaptist history could help the contemporary church deal with change.

Nonetheless, I was attracted to theology like a moth to a candle flame. At this time, my theological output consisted of several articles in *The Mennonite* or *The Gospel Herald*, periodicals of the two largest Mennonite denominations, on issues like dialogue with Catholics or understanding the book of Revelation, as well as one academic article that offered a Mennonite perspective on several doctrines. The article in *The Mennonite* served as one of the sources of VanderEnde's denunciation of me.

The academic article that VanderEnde targeted had originated as a presentation at a June 1983 conference on systematic theology at Associated Mennonite Biblical Seminaries. As far as I can determine, it was the first Mennonite conference to deal with theology as *systematic* theology. Previously, discussions of theology occurred under the rubric of "biblical." This conference took place in one room at AMBS, with perhaps fifteen people sitting around tables arranged in a square. There may have been one or two women among the majority of men in attendance. Men made all five presentations. I spoke last.

When Willard Swartley, professor of New Testament and chair of the meeting called on me, he said that Denny has a "different kind of paper." With that comment I realized that I had misread the purpose of the meeting, which was primarily to deal with methodology as Mennonites began to engage what for them was the new discipline of *systematic theology*. My paper offered statements on biblical authority, Christology, and atonement that reflected what I intended as a specifically Mennonite perspective set in a changing modern context. AMBS printed the presentations from this conference as number 7 in their series of *Occasional Papers*. My presentation in this printed form constituted the primary source of VanderEnde's ire. As I recall, he accused me of denying biblical infallibility and thus of misreading Anabaptists, who he said believed in biblical infallibility.

On a side note for later reference, the lack of women around the table in this 1983 conference on *systematic* theology indicates a problem still needing ongoing attention. Also, for later reference, two other presentations were by A. James Reimer, a professor of theology at Conrad Grebel College in Waterloo, Ontario, and Thomas Finger, at the time a theology professor at Northern Baptist Theological Seminary in Chicago. Reimer and Finger, along with myself, later emerged as the representative voices for three specific approaches to a theology for Mennonites or the peace church. Comments later in this memoir describe my conversations with Reimer and Finger.

This conference at Camp Wonderland was not my first interaction with Ted VanderEnde. A couple years earlier, Bluffton College president Elmer Neufeld, who wanted to position the college so that it could appeal to folks such as VanderEnde, had invited him to speak on campus two or three times.

At one point, VanderEnde had invited me to lunch for an extended conversation. He brought along his young assistant pastor Ted Kushel. We met at the longtime, iconic Ingalls restaurant on Main Street in Bluffton. VanderEnde indicated that we probably had different perspectives, but he expressed interest in learning my approach to religious authority and recent Anabaptist history. I felt honored that this pastor, who was a generation older than I, would want to know my views. He posed questions to draw me out. He claimed not to know about recent developments in Anabaptist history and asked for a bibliography that would bring him up to date. I left the conversation with the impression that although we saw things differently, we could agree to disagree. I was soon disabused of that idea.

The day after this lunchtime conversation, I had occasion to talk with C. J. Dyck, professor of Anabaptist and Mennonite history at AMBS. C. J. told me that VanderEnde had just taken a course on Anabaptist history at AMBS, and he already knew everything that he had quizzed me about. He was merely pushing me to see how far gone I was into the views that he rejected. In other words, I had naively fallen into a trap. This experience taught me to be more suspicious when people wanted to know what my perspectives are. And now at Camp Wonderland, I experienced the full force of my naïveté.

Break time came after VanderEnde's presentation. I went directly to him and to Vern Preheim, member of the planning committee and General Secretary of the General Conference Mennonite Church. I protested that it was unfair to single me out as the epitome of the "bad guys" at such an event without at least a prior warning and opportunity to respond. Vern said that I would have an opportunity for a response at the beginning of the session the next day. VanderEnde said that anything written was "fair game."

When the session resumed, Jake Elias, AMBS professor of New Testament, gave the formal response to VanderEnde. Jake paraphrased and restated some of my statements in a way to indicate that my views were not as bad as VanderEnde had indicated but did so gently so as not to appear to confront him directly. Clearly conservatives were to be handled with care. In the open discussion, some folks thanked VanderEnde, while other voices defended me. I could hardly wait until the session

ended and I could withdraw somewhere and figure out how to
respond.

Before this session, I was enjoying the day. The first speaker
had cited my article in *The Mennonite* very favorably, and during the break after that session, other folks had also thanked me
for it. After VanderEnde's attack, friends made a point of supporting me, saying that it was unfair to single me out for such an
attack. Others made jokes, such as "Oh, hi, Denny, I heard that
you were here."

The next day I was given an opportunity for a response. I
spoke for twenty minutes. I began with an affirmation on the importance of the Bible, which everyone could agree on. It is our
book and speaks about our spiritual origins and spiritual ances-
tors, I said. As my main point, I described two worldviews. One
assumed unchanging absolutes and resisted talking about diversity in the Bible, rejected higher criticism, assumed an unchanging theology, and more. The other worldview accepted change
and recognized that while there might be an absolute truth, no
human statement could contain it fully. Thus every statement of
theology was limited and contextual, and we needed to accept
the possibility of change. However, even as we accepted changing perspectives, such as process theology, each is still a finite
system and cannot be absolutized.

In my final point, I said that even as spokespeople for these
two worldviews made each other nervous, each was necessary—
one emphasized continuity with the past, which was important,
and the other focused on making the faith relevant in a modern
context, which was important. Finally I emphasized that while I
clearly adhered to the worldview that assumed change and could
use systems that assumed change, it was important to circum-
scribe those with a Mennonite agenda of Christocentric faith,
discipleship to Jesus Christ, the church as a community, and rejection of violence. I received many statements of thanks for my
response.

In following months, it became clear that my publications
were credible, and I received enough external support that President Neufeld defended me despite his generally conservative
orientation and fear that my writing would upset Evangelicals.

To protect Bluffton College from repeated attacks from conservative elements of the constituency, President Neufeld invited Vern Preheim, the General Secretary of the General Conference Mennonite Church, to meet with VanderEnde and me. As a result of this meeting VanderEnde agreed to cease printing his newsletter, in which he had published his broadside against me from the Camp Wonderland conference, as well as a second issue that contained what he considered additional, damaging material. On my part, I agreed not to write anything against VanderEnde. Thus public hostility would cease. Since it allowed me no published response to VanderEnde's printed comments, I was not entirely happy with that outcome, but the agreement held. It would still be a few years before I could encounter such an attack without being knocked off balance, and I could consider it merely the neo-Fundamentalist response that my theology elicited.

A subsequent action had greater and longer-term dimensions. Already in 1984, the Mennonite Church and the General Conference Mennonite Church had begun to discuss merger. To determine if a basis for merger existed, executives from each denomination put together a task force to write a confession of faith that each denomination could accept. With his profile, VanderEnde was placed on this task force, a move that assured the fundamentalists that their voices would be heard. This confession of faith was eventually approved by both denominations in 1995.

When Ted VanderEnde retired from St. John Mennonite Church, he and his wife moved back to the Netherlands. I never saw him again. In 2020 I published an article in *Anabaptist Witness*, the periodical of AMBS, in which I offered a major critique of the 1995 confession of faith. To me, it may have seemed like a last word to VanderEnde, but more importantly, the larger discussion continued.

11

Side Lines

I considered the essay that earned Ted VanderEnde's ire a deviation from my supposed real writing focus on early or sixteenth-century Anabaptist theology. However, that particular essay was not the only project that was taking me in new directions.

A major new initiative in Mennonite history posed an irresistible attraction. While I was still in graduate school, a years-long project was set in motion to write a history of the Mennonite Experience in America, often abbreviated as the MEA project. This project focused on the Mennonites in the United States, with scholars in Canada developing a Canadian parallel. Institutes and individuals from several Mennonite denominations donated funds for the project, while the Institute of Mennonite Studies at Associated Mennonite Biblical Seminaries administered the project.

Four epochs were identified—colonial period, nineteenth century, 1890-1930, and 1930 to the present, which at that time, would have been the 1970s—with an author identified for each epoch. In addition, to stimulate interest in the project and to develop additional material for the four volumes, colleges and historical societies were invited to sponsor conferences in which scholars presented relevant research.

The project soon caught me up. In the late 1970s, I had attended several conferences generated by this project, including one in Goshen, Indiana, another at Bethel College in North Newton, Kansas, and finally one based at Messiah College in

Grantham, Pennsylvania, and Mellinger's Mennonite Church in Lancaster, Pennsylvania. With such stimulation, I wanted to contribute academically to the conversation about Mennonites in the United States.

I outlined a project in early Mennonite theology that could constitute a C. Henry Smith Peace Lecture. C. Henry Smith taught history at Goshen and Bluffton colleges, and after his death, a trust was established with his estate. As one of the initiatives, the trust sponsors a lecture each year to be delivered on the two campuses by a faculty member from one of the named colleges. I applied for and received the Smith Lecture for the 1979-80 academic year.

For my lecture, I studied statements of atonement in several early nineteenth-century Mennonite writers. In the last half of this century, Mennonites began developing denominational structures, a publishing company, mission societies, periodicals and other changes parallel to developments in the wider society. In preparation for his volume in the Mennonites in America series, Theron Schlabach had described these changes as a "quickening" rather than as a fundamental change in direction. In my Smith lecture, I attempted to show that Schlabach's observation applied to theology as well. Using atonement image as a test case, I argued that Mennonites on either side of the quickening used versions of traditional satisfaction atonement imagery but did so with a distinct Mennonite dimension. Thus even though Mennonites were significantly influenced by American fundamentalism, they maintained their distinct identity as a peace church.

I presented this lecture in April 1980 at Bluffton College and in May at Goshen College. When I sought to publish the lecture, I received the suggestion to include more historical characters. I readily agreed, but it meant more research. A much longer essay was finally accepted for publication in August 1985, and a forty-page article appeared as "The Quickening of Soteriology" in the January 1987 issue of *Mennonite Quarterly Review*.

The project that became "The Quickening" was not the only thing I was working on at that time. I did manage to produce an article that analyzed atonement imagery in three sixteenth-cen-

tury figures—Martin Bucer, the reformation leader in Strasbourg, and Anabaptists Michael Sattler and Hans Denck. It was
published in *Mennonite Quarterly Review* with the title, "The
Work of Christ: The Difficulty of Identifying an Anabaptist Perspective," since Sattler's view of atonement resembled that of
Bucer's. I also had an idea for a similar analysis of Balthasar
Hubmaier and Hans Hut. However, that project waited several
years for development, and my work continued to deviate from
sixteenth-century Anabaptism.

In spring 1984, C. J. Dyck, church history professor at
AMBS, recommended me for a project that I was glad to accept.
Greenwood Press had initiated a publication series on American
denominations. They had written to C. J., who recommended
me to write the volume on the Mennonites. I was thrilled with
the opportunity. I signed a contract and received an advance of
$250.00.

Since my first sabbatical at Bluffton College was scheduled
to begin that fall, the invitation came at an opportune time. The
initial phase of writing fit with my supposed focus on early Anabaptists. I began writing what was intended to be a short history of the sixteenth-century story of Anabaptist origins as a
prelude to Mennonites in America. When I finally finished, I had
a computer printout of some ninety double-spaced pages, much
too long for the introduction to an American story. Abandoning
most of it and reducing this story to an acceptable five and at
most ten pages was out of the question. I decided to pursue publication of it as a stand-alone item.

My story of Anabaptism made use of new "polygenesis"
scholarship, which challenged an iconic view of Anabaptist origins. In 1975, an article by James Stayer, Werner Packull, and
Klaus Deppermann entitled "From Monogenesis to Polygenesis" provided a major revision of the understanding of origins,
directly challenging the view of Harold S. Bender, a past dean of
Goshen Biblical Seminary.

Bender outlined his view in two publications—his essay
"The Anabaptist Vision," whose first appearance was the 1942
presidential address to the American Society of Church History,
and his 1950 biography of Conrad Grebel. Appearing during

World War II, "Anabaptist Vision" served as the paradigm for Anabaptism as a Bible-based movement characterized by three emphases: following the example of Jesus Christ (discipleship), the church as a voluntary community distinct from the world, and nonresistance in all human relationships.

Bender wrote that Grebel had founded Anabaptism in Zurich, Switzerland, and that true Anabaptism descended from that single beginning point, in an unbroken line that continued down to Mennonites in North America. For Bender, this unbroken line served to exclude Thomas Müntzer, who had fomented revolution with peasants, and the revolutionary Anabaptists in the city of Münster. In contrast, the polygenesis story of pluralistic origins showed that Anabaptism originated independently in a least three separate locations, with little initial contact between them, and that Thomas Müntzer and the revolutionaries in Münster indeed belonged to the story.

In response to the 1975 article, some voices had appealed to the polygenesis story to argue that a pluralistic origin validated a pluralistic, contemporary church, including abandoning rejection of violence as a characteristic of the modern Mennonite church. I did not accept that interpretation. Along with my ninety-page historical summary, I wrote a chapter on the "meaning of Anabaptism" with my own application of the story. I argued that even amid pluralistic origins, early Anabaptists remained the origins of the contemporary peace church.

I submitted the manuscript to Herald Press, including the chapter on meaning. The wait for a decision was excruciating. In October 1985 I received the letter of acceptance. I could not have been happier. The one-time, much-expanded introduction to a proposed one-volume history of Mennonites became *Becoming Anabaptist*, my first book. It appeared early in 1987.

Meanwhile, I needed to keep working on a history of Mennonites in North America. With the material on sixteenth-century origins in hand, I developed an understanding of another important background story for Mennonites in North America. Large numbers of Mennonites in North America immigrated from Russia in several contingents in the late nineteenth- and early twentieth-centuries; this was the story I set out to develop.

It began with Dutch Anabaptist refugees from the Netherlands, who early on found a refuge in the area of Danzig and East Prussia. Eventually, when restrictions were placed on them, some of these Mennonites accepted the invitation of Tzarina Catherine the Great to move to the Ukrainian region of southern Russia. By 1789, hundreds of Mennonites were settling in what is now Ukraine. From there, immigration to North America began in the mid-1870s. Again, I developed a written account that was much too long for a story of Mennonites in North America.

Inevitably as I was drawn into the story of Mennonites in North America, I wanted to involve Bluffton College in the project. In July 1986 I secured permission from President Elmer Neufeld to organize a conference in Bluffton as part of the ongoing series of conferences on the Mennonite experience in America. The series had been advancing through the eras. By 1986 the primary focus was on experiences of Mennonites in the nineteenth century. Mennonites first settled in the Bluffton area in 1833. Before this, Mennonite immigrants from Switzerland and the Alsace region had settled in Pennsylvania in the early eighteenth century, and their descendants had moved west with the advancing European frontier.

In contrast, the Swiss Mennonite immigrants to the Bluffton area belonged to a contingent that settled in Ohio directly from Europe and thus had an identity distinct from the earlier Swiss immigrants. This arrival date and their distinct identity made it ideal to sponsor a conference that focused on the nineteenth-century Swiss immigrants to Ohio. The conference took place 5-7 November 1987.

With the approval for a conference in Bluffton, I wanted to have a part on our own program. Following my ongoing interest in atonement theology, I began a project that would compare and analyze atonement imagery for representatives of several different kinds of nineteenth-century Mennonite and Amish groups. One obvious choice was Johannes Moser, the first minister and bishop who served the Bluffton area Swiss Mennonite church from 1853 until his death in 1908. The other figures in my paper for the conference were Jacob Stauffer, a conservative

Mennonite minister in Lancaster, Pennsylvania, and Heinrich Egly, who led a progressive and revivalist-oriented Amish group in Illinois.

As I began this project for the November 1987 conference, I assumed that there would be little material and that I would write a short paper with a few indications of direction. This assumption proved incorrect in a big way. I found a great deal of material, more than I could process in a conference paper. For material on Johannes Moser, I sought advice from James O. Lehman, a descendant of the Ohio Swiss Mennonite immigrants and at that time librarian at Eastern Mennonite University. Lehman had written histories of several congregations of these Swiss immigrants in eastern Ohio. He suggested that I check the three articles that Johannes Moser had written on nonresistance in *Herald der Wahrheit*, the most important Mennonite periodical of the era.

Articles from Moser illustrate the wealth of material that I found for this project. The historical library of Bluffton University had copies of *Herold der Wahrheit*. I quickly found the three articles by Moser. Spreading the large, bound volume out on a library table in a quiet reading room, and reading his articles in a paper that he himself could have handled, gave me the sense of chatting with Moser. After reading the three articles to which I had been pointed, on a whim I turned a few pages and discovered another article by Moser, and a couple of pages later yet another one.

I decided that I should be systematic and thorough. I pulled the first volume of *Herald der Wahrheit*, which had been published in 1864, off the shelf. I started from the first issue and turned every page until it ceased publication in 1905. Further, when more progressive Mennonites began publication of the periodical *Christlicher Bundesbote* in 1882, I discovered that Moser had switched the majority of his writing to that outlet. In these two sources, I found sixty-four articles by Moser.

Apart from the three articles with which I began, this material constituted a theological resource previously unknown in the modern era. I soon became the only person alive who had read all the published articles of Bishop Johannes Moser. As the only such reader, I could then make jokes about how easy it was to become a "world's expert." Meanwhile, I developed a real affinity for the elderly bishop. I attended First Mennonite Church in Bluffton, one of four congregations derived from the original, large Swiss Mennonite church he had served as minister and bishop.

That intimacy was helped along by the fact that his great-grandson John attended church with me. John showed me the shelf of books from Johannes' library, and the foot-powered lathe on which he made hunting rifles for the community. Johannes' great-great-grandson lived in the bishop's house. Adjacent to the house, I saw the bishop's barn, with the beam that ran the length of the barn and displayed the bishop's axe marks. Not surprisingly, Johannes Moser became my favorite character of this extended project.

My reading of Johannes also challenged the usual assumption about his leadership. Since the Bluffton congregation was the last of the Swiss congregations to join the General Conference Mennonite Church, the most progressive of the major Mennonite denominations, the assumption had been that a conservative bishop Johannes had held them back. However, when it became clear that he shifted his publication efforts to the General Conference periodical, and when his articles displayed his support for such progressive issues as mission work and higher education, I developed the thesis that Johannes was a progressive bishop trying to convince a reluctant church to join the General Conference.

In any case, following the conference in November 1987, I started working toward publication of the presentation. Since it contained only three of a number of varieties of Amish and Mennonites, I added other examples to fill out the picture of the figures on whom I had already worked. This project grew ever larger.

As the project expanded, it came in conflict with the one-volume history that I was supposed to be writing on Mennonites in America. I had concluded that I should not rush through a manuscript when a wealth of original research was in process for a four-volume series on the Mennonites in America. Thus I was stalling and making excuses about delays to my editor while waiting on the coming original publications. In addition, I really wanted to focus on the manuscript that dealt with the variety of theological expressions in the nineteenth century. I decided that the project to write a one-volume history was untenable for me. I wrote a check for $250.00, returned my advance to the publisher, and resigned from the project. Freed, I threw myself into the nineteenth-century project, which was eventually published in 1997 as the book *Keeping Salvation Ethical*.

As I approached the mid-point of my career, I had spent more time working on issues in American Mennonite theology and history than I had in the Anabaptist era of the Reformation. Alongside this work on the theology of nineteenth-century Mennonite and Amish writers, I was also continuing to make progress on questions of Christology and atonement specifically for Mennonites or for the peace church. The move toward a new professional identity continued apace.

12

Activism

Since returning to the United States in 1970, I had been a proponent of nonviolent activism. In my classes, I talked about the theory of activism and posed it as an alternative to violence at levels from local to international. Since my activities against the Vietnam war during seminary, however, I had had little opportunity to engage in nonviolent activism. That situation changed with one letter, and in the follow-up, I learned several unexpected lessons.

The letter came from Gene Stoltzfus, whom I had known and liked since we both lived in Shoup House at Goshen College, and he had helped to teach me how to understand the creation stories in Genesis 1 and 2 and come to terms with evolution. Gene was the first director of the newly formed Christian Peacemaker Teams (more recently renamed Community Peacemaker Teams), often called CPT, a nonviolent activism and violence reduction organization originally sponsored by Mennonite, Brethren, and Quaker churches. Gene's letter invited me to be part of a CPT delegation that would travel to Haiti during Christmas vacation in December 1992.

In the letter and a follow-up phone call, Gene explained that since it would engage in activities in support of those the current Haitian government sought to oppress, the trip might involve some danger. A military junta had seized control of the government in a coup that had ousted the democratically elected president Jean Bertrand Aristide and appeared to have the support of the United States government. Aristide had been a justice-seeking, wildly popular president. He had received something like 65 percent of the vote in an election certified by foreign observers. The second-place candidate, the one backed by the United States, had received 15 percent of the vote. The government of the coup leaders was engaged in efforts to suppress the party of Aristide, and with many citizens in hiding, the CPT delegation would .express support for the people in hiding and confront the violence perpetrated by the government. To date, white people who engaged in protest activity had not been challenged, Gene said, but there was always a possibility that such protection might cease.

I talked about Gene's invitation at home and the danger it might involve. My wife and three daughters, the youngest of whom was now a college student, all encouraged me to go. Just the week before, I had talked about nonviolent activism in one of my classes. Such activism might involve some danger, I said, but people who professed faith in nonviolence should be willing to face that danger, just as people in the military willingly faced danger. It became clear to me that if I did not go to Haiti with CPT, I could never again talk about nonviolent activism in any of my classes.

Gene gave me a task in preparation for the delegation. I needed to raise $1000.00, which meant asking First Mennonite Church, my home congregation, for support money. I dreaded that task, but I did make a plea for money, and I received sufficient funds for the trip. Asking the congregation for money later emerged in an unexpected but helpful way.

The rule by the junta that ousted Aristide was repressive. Haitians were forbidden to meet in groups of more than four persons without an army permit. It was government policy to obliterate Lavalas, the movement that had brought Aristide to the office of President. It was illegal to say the name of Lavalas, and people who mentioned Lavalas or Aristide in public were subject to arrest. Or they just disappeared in the night. More than once our little group of North Americans was cautioned not to mention the names of Aristide and Lavalas when walking in the street, lest we bring suspicion on the Haitians walking with us.

Of a total population of 6 million, an estimated 250,000 Aristide supporters had gone underground rather than risk death at the hands of the army. Most of those in the underground had come to the attention of the army because they had worked publicly for Lavalas or had worked in social programs organized by Lavalas to address such needs as literacy or the fair sale of crops. Many had left their homes precipitously, slipping out a back way when friends or family came to warn them of army personnel approaching their houses.

Our delegation spent a week talking with people in the underground to hear their stories and to give them a voice. One part of our mission was to gather stories that we could tell back in the US to give visibility to the problems. The hope was that exposing this violence to the light of day might unleash forces of change. In these conversations, we thought of the folks at home who had contributed money for the trip. Those thoughts made it very real to tell the Haitians that many people in the United States knew about their plight.

Another part of our mission was to engage in public action that would speak for the suppressed and oppressed people of Haiti. As we prepared for our day of public actions, the Haitians in the guest house where we stayed were thrilled to see us off—we would engage in activities on their behalf that would be dangerous for them to participate in. We went to the US embassy carrying a statement that described the oppression of the population being carried out by the government of the junta that the US appeared to support. We handed the statement through a locked gate to a low-level functionary who promised that her superiors would give it careful consideration.

We had invited Haitian TV stations to film us outside the US embassy. Protected by our status as whites and foreigners, and in full view of Haitian TV cameras, members of our delegation read statements from people hiding in the underground. One was an eloquent call for Haitians and foreigners alike to continue to struggle nonviolently for justice in Haiti.

From the embassy, we traveled to a statue in the heart of Port-au-Prince that symbolized Haitian freedom. It was a larger-than-life image of a slave blowing a conch shell to call slaves to revolution. The statue recalled the series of uprisings that began in 1791 against colonialists and colonial occupiers Britain and France. These risings culminated with the formation of an independent Haiti in 1804, the first nation founded by former slaves. In close view in one direction from this statue stood the army headquarters, with soldiers visible on a second-floor balcony. Perhaps ninety degrees to the right, at about the same distance stood the capitol building. These two buildings housed the symbolic actors of the oppressive forces that our delegation was in Haiti to protest.

The delegation clasped hands and formed an uneven circle around this statue that symbolized freedom. In that circle our delegation recited a liturgy, sang several songs, and prayed together. As someone prayed aloud, it took a couple moments before I realized that another voice was speaking beside me—by my right hand. I turned and saw an elderly Haitian man, who had to repeat his quiet, labored English words a couple times before they sank in. He said only, "When I hear you praying, I have hope. When I hear you praying, I have hope." As this elderly gentleman's words penetrated my consciousness, the reality of what we were doing flashed over me.

The elderly gentleman sensed it before I did. His experience of hope revealed to me in a new and profound way the significance of our action. I had gone to Haiti to engage in political protest, and I was not particularly interested in engaging in public worship. Of course it was important to witness against injustice and oppression and to give voice to oppressed Haitians—and there is none of our political protesting that I would eliminate. But the elderly gentleman opened my eyes to see that we were also doing it as Christians, as God's people—and that was crucial.

We were engaged in a symbolic protest against violent injustice. But when I heard the elderly gentleman's words, I realized that we were more than a political protest. For a brief moment, in our circle the reign of God actually *was* present. Our group was the shalom community of God's people, making visible and present God's peace and salvation in contrast to the oppressive powers resident in the capitol building and army headquarters in full view across the avenues. For a brief moment, our circle was *more* than a symbol: in the hope expressed by the elderly Haitian man, I saw that the future reign of God *was* tangibly present and breaking into our world, and I experienced it. The elderly man had felt that peace and in his words he led me to experience it as well.

Those of us gathered in that circle were there because we were Christians committed to nonviolence. We expressed our solidarity with suffering people and gave an important political witness against real injustice. But it was more than a political protest. It was also making present the peaceable reign of God on the doorsteps of those who perpetrated violence and injustice.

This experience in Haiti changed the way that I understood nonviolent activism. It is a political action, and it is also more. It is the present in-breaking of the future, peaceable reign of God. It is also an image of what the church should be—a lived, visible expression of God's future salvation breaking into the present, even if it is not fully realized in Haiti or our own nation or anywhere else.

13

Normal '89

It was the Consultation on Christology, scheduled to coincide with the national gatherings of Mennonite Church and General Conference Mennonite Church in August 1989 on the campus of Illinois State University. As the book of papers and findings explained, the conference followed up conversations on Christology and its missionary implications among Mennonite and Brethren in Christ mission agencies at the 1984 Strasbourg Mennonite World Conference. Representatives from the Mennonite Church, the General Conference Mennonite Church, the Mennonite Brethren, and the Brethren in Christ planned the consultation that took place in Normal, Illinois, on the campus of Illinois State University.

Decked out in sport coat and tie, a couple cuts above my routine classroom garb of blue jeans and rugby shirts, I was feeling the good kind of nervous that meant I was alert and confident. As I approached the room for my first session, I was naively proud to be included in a major, churchwide event,

After all, I had two things going for me. For one, I had earlier asked Erland Waltner, program committee chair and president of the General Conference Mennonite side of Associated Mennonite Biblical Seminaries in Elkhart, Indiana, if there were any red flags in my paper. Erland had assured me that there were none. Further, going down the hill to the building for my session, I had crossed paths with Marlin Miller, president of the Mennonite Church half of AMBS in Elkhart. The papers to be discussed were distributed ahead of time, and as we passed,

Marlin had said, "Good paper." With Marlin's affirmation, I thought, "What can go wrong?" As I soon learned, the answer was "a whole session."

Christology is the part of theology that talks about how to identify and describe Jesus. The consultation did not arise in a vacuum. Its immediate context was the controversy swirling around Norman Kraus' recent publication of the book *Jesus Christ Our Lord*. Mennonite fundamentalist George R. Brunk II created the controversy with a loud and vociferous condemnation of the book as heretical. In Brunk's view, Kraus' language abandoned the deity of Christ.

Although I still considered myself a Reformation and early Anabaptism scholar, I developed a proposal for a paper for the August 1989 consultation. I wrote one letter to Erland Waltner, program committee chair, and offered a paper. He accepted my proposal. Apart from a response paper to A. James Reimer in a consultation at Conrad Grebel College, and a presentation at the Mennonite session at the annual meeting of the American Academy of Religion, this paper for the Normal '89 consultation was my second major entry in the discussion of theology for Mennonites.

My minimal first effort in systematic theology had come six years earlier, at the Colloquium on Systematic Theology at AMBS in June 1983. One version of my presentation from that colloquium was published in the series of Occasional Papers by AMBS and another version as "Perspectives on a Mennonite Theology" in the Fall 1984 issue of *Conrad Grebel Review*. As related in a previous chapter, the version in *Occasional Papers* provoked an eruption by Pastor Ted VanderEnde. My entry into the Normal '89 conversation was more audacious and apparently more provocative than I realized.

For Normal '89, I had proposed a paper that would correlate historically the acceptance of the sword by the church following Emperor Constantine's espousal of Christianity in 313 CE with the formulas that emerged from the Councils of Nicea (325 CE) and Chalcedon (451 CE). Constantine convoked the Council of Nicea, which declared Jesus "one in substance" or "one in being" with God, a formula restated by the Council of Constantinople

(381 C.E.), and which enshrined it in the form still used today as the Nicene Creed. The Council of Chalcedon followed up by applying Nicea's language for Jesus and God to Jesus and humanity, producing the formula that Jesus was "fully human and fully God."

My argument was that since these formulas lacked significant ethical content, they reflect the church of Constantine, namely the church that had accepted the sword. With the absence of any explicit ethical dimension in these conciliar statements, in essence their generic categories of "humanity" and "God" allowed Christians to profess faith in Jesus Christ the God-man while simultaneously espousing the sword that Jesus rejected. In my view, this acquiescence to the sword raised a question about the suitability of these conciliar statements as the foundation of theology for the peace church that followed Jesus in rejecting the sword.

I was mildly surprised that Erland accepted the paper. I thought that I was proposing an argument already articulated by John Howard Yoder, the most widely known Mennonite theologian and ethicist of that era. My naiveté and theological inexperience were showing. It was some years later before I realized that I was already going beyond Yoder. He had relativized the conciliar formulas in *Preface to Theology*, but he had not followed up by articulating the correlation that I was pointing out.

The consultation format called for finished papers to be distributed to participants ahead of time. At the consultation, each author would then have two sessions in which interested people could ask questions and discuss the papers. The room for my session was a typical university classroom—well-lighted from windows and overhead, fluorescent lights. It had perhaps six rows of chairs with arms, seating for about seventy-five students.

Forty-four people attended this first session. In the front row sat Ron Sider and Tim Epp. Epp was unknown to me at that point, though I soon learned that he was a fundamentalist Mennonite Brethren pastor from western Canada currently pastor of the conservative First Mennonite Church in Berne, Indiana. Sider was the well-known Evangelical who wrote about his

Evangelical Christian approach to economic issues and was founder and president of Evangelicals for Social Action. President Elmer Neufeld had invited Sider to Bluffton University a few months earlier to give the C. Henry Smith Peace lecture. While he was in Bluffton, I had broached a bit of the atonement theology I was thinking about, and Sider had agreed with me that Christus Victor was best suited for a communal dimension in atonement imagery. I assumed that Sider was a friendly face and Epp was unknown to me. The onslaught to follow thus caught me entirely unaware.

For the entire session, the conversation was dominated by Sider and Epp. It was not a friendly domination. They rejected my analysis outright. For the next hour, they expended great effort and posed a wide range of questions, all designed to get me to say something that they could openly condemn as unacceptable. I quickly realized that I should admit as little as possible, and that I would refuse to agree with whatever formula they wanted me to endorse. I also realized that there were nuances of doctrinal analysis that I needed to learn.

I am no longer sure of my responses, but I think that one of them was a refusal to agree that the essence or the "stuff" of God from an upper realm had come down and lived on earth for a while before returning to the heavenly realm. I have often wished that I could go through this session again. With hindsight, I imagine being able to push them back on their heels by posing questions they could not satisfactorily answer. Why, for example, should our theology today be limited by terminology from the fourth and fifth centuries that reflected long-discarded philosophical assumptions and was located in a three-decker worldview abandoned long ago?

By chance an acquaintance of mine sat directly behind Sider and out of his view, a position from which he gave me nods and fist shakes as I responded to Sider. It was a blessed relief when the session ended. I walked out dazed, unnerved, and unstrung. I had to walk around to collect myself. It was an effort to gear up for the next session. I approached it with fear and trembling.

When I entered the room for my second session, inside, my hands were raised mentally in a defensive posture of "Don't hit me." There were perhaps thirty people in the room. Seated in the front row was Millard Lind, professor of Old Testament at AMBS, and my favorite professor from my years as a student there. Again, I was unprepared for what happened next.

As the session began, I smiled warily, expecting another onslaught. But Millard expressed agreement with my paper, as did others in the room. Since there were no disagreements, the discussion actually lagged as participants sought questions to ask and comments to make. I walked out perplexed, wondering what to make of the day.

The following day, I attended the meeting of the findings committee, which gave me a different view of my paper. Here the opinion was offered that my paper should have been presented in a plenary session rather than being relegated to one of the break-out sessions. Informally, a number of people said that my paper should have been the keynote address for the entire Christology conference. It defined the real issues to be debated, I heard.

Erland Waltner edited all the papers from the consultation, along with responses, into a small book, *Jesus Christ and the Mission of the Church*. Tom Finger, at that time a Visiting Professor of Theology at Eastern Mennonite Seminary, wrote the response to my paper. It was my first experience with his unique methodology, which was to retain the classic language but to redefine it or fill the classic language with terms from elsewhere. In his view, this approach allowed him to agree with both sides, in this case classic Christology and also Anabaptist-Mennonite discipleship.

In my response, which I had to insist that Waltner include, I pointed out the paradox of Finger's hybrid view. The higher the value he placed on the classic creedal language he wanted to retain, the more problematic it became that it leaped from Jesus' birth to his death and separates ethics from Christology. Thus to save this language it was also necessary to make it lesser by proclaiming its incompleteness and then to redefine it in terms of Anabaptist-Mennonite discipleship. To me it was an unstable formula, which claimed that the classic language was simultaneously high and low.

After I left Normal, Ron Sider was not finished with me. A few days after I returned to Bluffton, I received a carbon copy of a letter that Sider had written to Erland Waltner. The letter mildly chastised Erland for putting me on the program after I had begged, and Sider concluded with the claim that I was dangerous and should be avoided.

I sent Sider a reply. I explained I had not begged; I had written only one letter to offer a paper. I also provided some additional explanation. Sider replied with a letter that expressed the equivalent of "Yes, better, but. . . ."

I waited for Erland to defend me. After all, he had assured me that there were no red flags in my paper. But what I got was a copy of a letter from Erland to Sider in which Erland said that he agreed with Sider in stressing the "biblical view." I felt betrayed by the man who had told me that my paper had "no red flags." At that time I was still unsure enough in the realm of theology that I said nothing to Erland.

My experience at Normal '89 still occupied my mind when a few months later, I received the invitation to spend the year as a Visiting Professor of Theology at Canadian Mennonite Bible College (now Canadian Mennonite University) in Winnipeg, Manitoba. The year in Winnipeg at CMBC is its own story, told in the following chapter, but one item relates to my experience at Normal '89. With the Sider-Epp attacks still front and center in my mind, I went to CMBC with the assumption that I needed to be very careful about what I said. Naively, I thought that they would not know about Sider's attack that had accused me of heresy.

At CMBC, the faculty had lunch together every day. Early in my time, the topic of Christology and the consultation at Normal '89 came up, and someone made a positive comment about my paper, even that it may have been the best of the papers presented. I mentioned that Ron Sider had not liked it. It turned out that at Normal '89, Sider had also attacked a CMBC faculty member who had contributed a paper. It quickly became apparent that Sider's actions at Normal '89 did not enthuse them. I relaxed. I knew I would have a good year at CMBC!

At the time, Normal '89 was an important event for me, namely to be included in a central theological discussion of the denomination. The response jolted me. In retrospect, I see other dimensions. For one, in later years I could begin to understand how threatening my views might seem to folks like Sider and Epp, who from my vantage point seemed to consider the conciliar statements to be transcendently true, unquestioned givens, elevated above historical contingency. For them, the argument that in other contexts and worldviews there could be alternative ways to respond to the issues addressed by the councils seemed to carry little weight.

When the conciliar terms are elevated to the status of transcendent, unquestioned givens, other answers are not possible. For those who embrace such transcendence, relativizing the conciliar statements appears to challenge the deity of Jesus and even the basis of salvation itself. I do not sympathize with that argument, but I understand it.

When I recall that I waited for Erland Waltner to defend me, I see that at that point I was still expecting defense and validation to come from others. One of my learnings from this experience was not to expect anyone, particularly from the evangelical or conservative side, to speak up in my defense. At that point, I still had to learn to assert myself theologically. Many times since then, I have wished that I could play this entire experience again, challenge Sider more astutely, and question Erland's response to Sider. In at least one account to follow, I did indeed stand up for myself, and I have been grateful for the many colleagues who have supported my views.

CASTLE

14

The Year that Might Not Have Been

The invitation to move to Winnipeg, Manitoba, Canada, for a year as a Visiting Professor of Theology at then Canadian Mennonite Bible College (CMBC) and now Canadian Mennonite University, came as a total shock—but it triggered one of the most formative and enriching years of my career. Mary and I and our youngest daughter Michelle lived in Winnipeg from August 1990 to July 1991. I learned much both inside and outside my classroom. Given how much that learning contributed to my life and career, it is sobering and even frightening to think how close it came to not happening.

On the basis of this experience, I changed my professional identity. In the evening phone call with the invitation, Dean Gerald Gerbrandt asked me to teach "theology," which I did not consider my discipline. In my mind, I had been dabbling in theology. *Becoming Anabaptist* still had the aura of a recent publication, and I continued to consider myself a church historian and Anabaptist scholar. During the year in Winnipeg, however, I decided that I should live up to expectations. If they thought that I knew enough theology to be listed as a professor of theology, then I decided to call myself a theologian. And one way or another, I have been a theologian ever since.

The invitation was exhilarating. It was a real charge to learn that another institution wanted me and that they had evidently noticed and valued the writing that I had been doing. That sense of being wanted posed something of a contrast to vibes I got from my own president, Elmer Neufeld. On occasion he let me know that my writing caused him problems with the conservative constituency that he wanted to court.

It was with significant satisfaction then, that I could march into his office the next morning to proclaim that someone valued me and to ask permission to spend a year in Canada. The president seemed eager to say "yes," explaining that "it would be good for you." It was like he was encouraging me to go. Only later did I develop enough insight into how administrators work to realize that Dean Gerbrandt would have asked the president for permission to talk to me, and thus the president knew what I would say the minute I appeared in his office door.

The invitation was scary. I knew little about CMBC. I assumed that it was a relatively conservative institution. As the previous chapter recounted, only a few months earlier, I had been loudly and publicly challenged by conservative-leaning Ron Sider and Tim Epp. I feared that CMBC might discover what I really was—and withdraw the invitation. But as I explained, they knew all about that noisy challenge, and they actually approved of my views!

CMBC was a teaching center of the University of Manitoba. In addition to graduating from CMBC, students could count their hours from CMBC toward a degree from the University. Because of the affiliation, I had a University of Manitoba faculty card. I drove over there to play handball with a grad student and a faculty member. I even had a letter to the editor published in *The Manitoban*, the university's newspaper.

The teaching entailed a lot of work, but I increased my knowledge of contemporary theology greatly. It was not an exaggeration to begin calling myself a theologian that year! In the initial phone conversation, Dean Gerbrandt listed three courses I would teach each semester. One was a course of my choice—meaning that I could teach one of my Bluffton courses. A second would be a course in which the students and I would read a theology book together and discuss it—and I could handle that easily. The third course was their standard, introductory theology course. The text book was one that I knew, plus a "few other small things," the dean added as a seeming afterthought. Since I knew the basic text, I assumed that I could handle that course as well. However, when I actually began reading the "few other things," it turned out to be seven books. I did work quite hard. These books were all new to me, which meant that I force-fed myself a great deal of theology that was new to me.

CMBC had fourteen faculty and about 150 students. Bluffton College had about 750 students, and I was part of a two-person department, with perhaps a dozen majors and minors. These figures produced an interesting juxtaposition of perceptions. Although Bluffton was a small college, to the fourteen faculty of CMBC, it seemed big. The CMBC faculty called themselves a small institution vis-à-vis the University of Manitoba. However, since I could talk with any of the faculty about my discipline and all the students were in religion classes, with reference to Bluffton College, CMBC felt to me like a huge department.

The perception of belonging to a huge department also caused me a problem with the introductory course. Since all students were in religion classes, I assumed that they were already knowledgeable. I went too fast and hit subjects too lightly. There were complaints. The dean had to remind me that they might all be religion students, but they were beginners in this introductory class, and I needed to approach them as such. After that conversation, things went better.

In Winnipeg, I picked up valuable material for my book manuscript on the views of atonement theology in a variety of nineteenth-century Mennonite and Amish traditions. Winnipeg is the locus of the largest number of late nineteenth- and early twentieth-century Russian Mennonite refugees from Ukraine in North America. I was able to develop my understanding of this facet of Mennonite history. Through consultation with colleagues in Winnipeg, I identified a conservative, Old Colony Mennonite preacher from the late nineteenth-century immigrants who became the eighth and final addition to the outline of the project that became *Keeping Salvation Ethical*. These were valuable learnings

Outside the confines of CMBC, I learned a lot about Canada. Like many Americans, I moved to Canada with the assumption that it was a friendly extension of the United States, virtually a fifty-first state. I was quickly disabused of these assumptions. I learned that Canada is a foreign country, with different ways of thinking and talking and operating. For example, in politics, I learned that most of my friends were Grits, a popular name for the Liberal Party, with a few NDPs, and no Tories, and that the Tory MP of my riding was the PM of Manitoba, but local Tories differed from national Tories.

I learned that the ethos of Canada exudes and breathes hockey in a way that surpasses any potential parallel in the United States, even NFL football. Thus I learned that when I had a difficult problem, I could "stick handle" my way through it. I also learned that professional football in Canada—the CFL—was a more wide-open game with more ways of scoring and was thus more interesting than the United States' NFL, the "*No Fun League*."

I learned that even when they may like individuals from the United States, Canadians were not particularly fond of the United States as a country because of its dominance and ignorance of Canada. When I watched TV, I got a glimpse of why. NBC's *Today* Show was readily available in Winnipeg, and I watched for some news of "home." But even though it was shown in Canada, the weather maps never even showed the border lines for the Canadian provinces, and weather forecasters never mentioned Canada except as the source of "a Canadian cold air mass." One of my friends told me that if he wanted a cheap laugh in class, he just told an anti-American joke. As a sample joke, consider this faux quote attributed to unpopular Prime Minister Brian Mulroney: "I have been busy, I was on the phone all afternoon agreeing with George Bush." By the time I left Canada, I was laughing right along with the Canadians!

Living in Canada that year was an eye-opening and enriching social experience as well as shifting my professional identity to theologian, and contributing to one of my important book projects. But with a different answer to one particular question, the year in Canada would not have happened. Given the wealth of experiences I gained from a jam-packed year, it is sobering and shocking to think what I would have missed with a different

answer to one particular question. When I asked Dean Gerbrandt about texts for the introductory course, had he given me
the titles of those seven additional books in addition to the main
text, I would have told him that I could not possibly do it.

THREE
MIDDLE GAME

15

Arrived

The year in Winnipeg came at the midpoint of my teaching career. In a sense, it also constituted a beginning. I returned from Canadian Mennonite Bible College calling myself a theologian for the first time, and eager to embrace this new identity. I entered theological conversations, developed positions, and learned much, some of which came the hard way.

One of the first conferences I attended with my new identity as theologian was in October 1991, just a couple months after returning from Winnipeg. The conference carried the title "Women Doing Theology." It dealt with issues of violence against women and the problems of a hierarchical church. Associated Mennonite Biblical Seminaries hosted the conference, with plenary sessions meeting in the Chapel of the Sermon on the Mount. Women planned the program, and all speakers were women. Since these were Mennonite women, I knew many of those involved with the planning and on the program. As a "theologian," I was anxious to attend a theology conference.

Perhaps 120 participants gathered in the chapel for the opening session, the majority women but some men scattered throughout. On the first day, I did general networking, which is a valuable dimension of conference attendance, but said nothing in the plenary discussion periods. In my assigned small group, women pointed out that women did theology differently than men—women wanted to tell stories and start with their feelings while men made abstract statements.

It was the second day of the conference where my real learning happened. In the first session of the day, Ruth Krall, a professor at Goshen College, said that western theology is patriarchal and hierarchical, which reinforces male dominance, culminating in rape. She called for the abandonment of patriarchal and masculine theology. She also explained that a rapist coerces obedience when he threatens to kill the victim if she tells. If the victim remains silent, she is changed by her coerced obedience.

In the discussion period, I offered a comment and asked a question. I said that I agreed with the call to reject hierarchical and patriarchal theology, but going a step farther that I was also bothered by the Mennonite emphasis on discipleship understood as "obedience to a male Jesus." "So," I asked, "did she have any suggestions for dealing with the obedience theme?" The session was also located in the Chapel of the Sermon on the Mount. On the wall, a few feet from the speaker, hangs a carved, wooden, art piece with the unpunctuated statement "thy kingdom come thy will be done on earth as it is in heaven," the single, New-Testament text most associated with obedience. That setting might seem an ironic place to challenge concepts of hierarchy and obedience.

I thought that I would be thanked for supporting Krall's position and furthering the discussion. That was a serious miscalculation. Not only was I not thanked for my agreement, she refused to answer my question. "You will have to think about it for yourself," she said. I tried again, saying that I had already written something on that theme, but I wanted to know what she thought. Again, she replied, "I won't answer that. You will just have to think about it for yourself."

I sat down, perplexed, wishing I could disappear, feeling a hundred pairs of eyes fixed on me. Other questions followed from women, but I recall nothing from the remainder of the session. I do recall the immediate aftermath.

When the session terminated, I was standing by my chair, wondering if anyone would speak to me, when I spied a determined-looking woman I did not know bearing down on me. She did not introduce herself, but eyed me fiercely. "Denny," she

said, "as long as you men keep reinforcing the hierarchy, we cannot even talk to you." I protested that I had agreed with the
speaker in rejecting hierarchy. She replied that as long as I was
using the term *obedience*, I was reinforcing hierarchy. When I
asked what language I should be using, she refused to answer.
"You would just use your male categories to say that I am
wrong," she said. She walked away, leaving me more perplexed
than ever.

For me, the redeeming feature of the conference was the
small group to which I was assigned. I went to the next session of
the small group both eager and fearful to hear what the women
in the group would tell me about what had just happened. One
participant in the group was Betty Sommer, a Bluffton College
Professor of Social Work, and a member of my Sunday school
class at First Mennonite Church. My familiarity with Betty was
both welcome and frightening. Betty and the other women did
not pull any punches.

The women in the group told me that I had misread and misunderstood what was happening, in the room, and in this conference. I needed to understand, they said, that this was the first
event in which women were fully in charge and could find their
voices and speak without a man lording it over them. Thus my
intervention in the discussion was simply inappropriate. This
was a women's meeting, and I was not perceptive enough to see
that.

Further, when I said that I had thought about the question
but wanted to know what Krall thought, that was just another instance of a man saying that he already knew the answer and
wanting to know if the woman was smart enough to agree with
him. I was just the typical man who could not let a problem lie
there and allow women to express their feelings. I had to jump in
and try to fix the problem that I implied I had already figured
out. The fact that I was merely curious and did not mean to up-
stage Krall was irrelevant. I should have sensed the moment and
not even asked the question.

Since I had lived with four assertive women—my wife and
three daughters—I knew enough to listen to the explanation by
the women in my group. They were correct, of course. I recalled

the first conference on systematic theology at AMBS in 1983, only eight years earlier. At that time, perhaps fifteen men met in a classroom, and all presentations were by men. Now in 1991, 120 women met in the chapel with a program organized and presented by women. It was a remarkable development, but I needed a jolt to recognize its significance.

By the time I got to the afternoon session, I knew my role was to listen. When the leader of the session announced that the women valued the presence of the men and thus asked the men to participate with their silence, I had already realized that I would not say another word.

At this conference I received a rude awakening—but I deserved it. Perhaps the most important point I learned was the significance of perspective and context, and that perspective and context applied both to the immediate situation and to the long-standing milieu from which theology emerged. I learned that women stood at a different place and brought a different context than I did when it came to doing theology. This learning changed the way that I read the writing of women. Rather than wandering around before they got to the point, as I had thought, I learned that many women told stories to anchor their theology because they needed to establish a social location for their thought different from that of traditional, presumed male, abstract theology. This awareness of context was also learning that I could then apply to my eventual encounters with black and womanist theology. Those stories are still to come in this memoir.

Meanwhile, in late April 1992 I drove to Conrad Grebel College in Waterloo, Ontario for the second conference of Women Doing Theology. As an eager theologian, I assumed that I needed to know what was going on in all areas of Mennonite theology. This time, however, I went to the conference knowing that I would say nothing and work on listening. Even in my small group, I sat silent until specifically asked to speak.

At this conference, I was one of two men present. The second was a friend I had learned to know in Winnipeg. I also received a minor accolade. One of the participants told me that she sympathized with the rough time I had had at the previous conference, and she thanked me for having the courage to attend this one and to stay in the conversation.

Bluffton College, my own institution, hosted the third such conference. I had no role in the planning, but I did attend. I was generally welcomed but did not speak publicly.

I did have one frustrating conversation at the Bluffton conference. After an evening session, standing at the bottom of the stairs in Marbeck Center, on the edge of the dining room, I chatted with a woman who had read an article I had written. She told me that she could tell I was trying, but I still was not really getting it. I implored her to teach me, to be more specific, to educate me on what I was missing. She refused. "You need to figure it out for yourself," she said, ending the conversation.

Learning to understand feminist theology was not easy. Even now I make no claim that I fully understand it. Nonetheless, this abrupt introduction to contemporary contexts was a valuable lesson that would serve well in learning from other theologies written by people who do not look like me or who live in a different cultural or ethnic context.

In March 1992 I attended a gathering at Laurelville Mennonite Church Center that was billed as a conversation with J. Lawrence Burkholder. The focus was a recognition and celebration of the long-delayed publication of Burkholder's dissertation. I was asked to give one of the responses. Several aspects of this conference had long-term implications for me.

Burkholder was fully aware of the nonresistant tradition in which both he and I had grown up. As I had done, he also moved away from it, embracing the nonviolent activism of the civil rights movement and Martin Luther King Jr. Where I disagreed with Burkholder was in the assessment of King's nonviolent activism. In articulating my disagreement with Burkholder, I developed a new paradigm that would serve me well in later years.

Burkholder pictured nonviolent resistance as a compromise, a halfway point between biblical nonresistance and effective violence. In other words, between true-but-ineffective nonresistance and effective violence, nonviolent resistance was described as a tool that employed a limited amount of violence to accomplish some good. I objected to calling nonviolent resistance and nonviolent activism a compromise and the exercise of some violence. Here for the first time I developed a model for responding to the idea that nonviolent activism and nonviolent resistance were using violence.

If nonviolent resistance is a form of violence, that means that there is a single continuum running from passive nonresistance at one end to great violence at the other extreme. Intermediary positions then identify different levels of violence. In essence, this continuum is defined by violence, and every position on it is some level of violence. Even giving a child a time out that opposed the child's will becomes a very short step along this continuum toward great violence.

My realization was that there are in fact two continua, both of which begin with nonresistance. The second continuum is defined by the refusal to commit harm or to use lethal violence. The positions on this continuum then depict actions that raise the intensity but do not cause damage and death. Examples might range from gentle persuasion to lawsuits to public protests to blocking traffic on streets and highways to massive demonstrations. In future contexts, this model of two continua became a useful argument. This discussion of the continua and other major presentations from the consultation were published in a book called *The Limits of Perfection*.

Another respondent to Burkholder was A. James Reimer, well known for advocating that theology for Mennonites should stand on the Nicene Creed and embrace classic Nicene-Chalcedonian and trinitarian orthodoxy. Reimer and I had previously exchanged sharp disagreements in writing. The Weaver-Reimer conversation was a known entity among Mennonite theologians.

For Mennonites, Reimer advocated a foundation in Nicene orthodoxy versus my argument that Nicea reflected the accommodation of the sword by the church after Constantine and that theology for Mennonites would be better served by a theology that began with the narrative of Jesus and bypassed Nicea and Chalcedon. The heart of the disagreement concerned the extent to which the classic creedal language constituted unquestioned givens, valid in all times and places, or were rather contingent statements that could be bypassed in other contexts.

An additional element of the Burkholder conversation was autobiographical statements by respondents. Reimer's story clearly established the reason for his commitment to Catholic Nicene orthodoxy. His parents came from two different conservative Mennonite traditions, one of which was revivalist. He went forward several times in revival meetings. Eventually he became disillusioned with what he experienced as an unstable Mennonite environment with little theological validity in the small Mennonite village in which he grew up. After a period of unbelief, he found faith again when he encountered Catholics during his university years. In contrast to Mennonite instability, he found a firm foundation in the unchanging Nicene Creed. In a sense, his salvation depended on finding that unchanging anchor outside of or beyond Mennonite tradition. I understood how his story shaped his approach to theology but I did not accept the conclusion he drew from it.

In my autobiographical statement, I described growing up as a Mennonite, pacifist minority in a world that knew almost nothing about Mennonites. Since I had learned that the pacifist church was a minority church, producing a theology for the peace church that would challenge the large, standard edifice of classic theology seemed like a normal activity. When I started to do theology, I was working to produce a theology that would buttress a minority, pacifist tradition in the wider world, as a counter to violence accommodating, standard or classic traditions. In contrast to Reimer's effort to find theological validity outside of Mennonite tradition, my search was to defend the theological validity of the Anabaptist-Mennonite tradition, which in my view emphasized building theology and ethics on the narrative of Jesus.

At this conference, I had a first conversation with Gerald Biesecker-Mast (now Gerald J. Mast), a graduate student in rhetoric at the University of Pittsburgh. During the social hour after Reimer's session, Gerald called me aside. I saw a typical graduate student, clad in deep brown corduroy sport coat, open collar shirt, round face with dark hair and dark-rimmed glasses. As we sipped juice and munched cookies, Gerald related that he was a follower of my direction for Mennonite theology. "If we follow Jim Reimer's line," he said, "there is not any reason left to be Mennonite." This conversation resembled any number of others that I had at conferences with graduate students and professors alike. At the time, neither of us could have any idea what this conversation foreshadowed for us in coming years.

The next January, Gerald arranged an invitation for me to speak at Pittsburgh Mennonite Church, where he attended while studying at the University of Pittsburgh. I preached and answered questions in a Sunday school class. As I recall, there was much anticipation for the inauguration of Bill Clinton as President. I said that I also supported Clinton, but I cautioned that since the reign of God was not identified with a political party, it had not come closer because Democrats had won. Gerald agreed.

I learned that Gerald grew up in a conservative Mennonite congregation in eastern Ohio and had attended Malone College. As.Gerald related, on the basis of reading John Howard Yoder's *The Politics of Jesus* and then my *Becoming Anabaptist*, he decided that Anabaptism provided the basis for a contemporary, nonviolent church that engaged the world and that he could live in. In graduate school, he brought his interest in communication together with a commitment to Anabaptism by writing a dissertation on sixteenth-century Anabaptist rhetoric around issues of nonviolence and the sword. Thus in Pittsburgh, Gerald asked me a lot of questions about my understanding of Anabaptism. Still nothing indicated that these ideas and the dissertation would grow into more significant parts of our relationship in coming years.

In 1987, Bluffton college received a grant from the Lilly Endowment for faculty development. Under the direction of the dean, Arden Slotter, the money was used to form the Bluffton College Study Center, a structure for awarding small, summer grants to support research by faculty. The first year, Robert Kreider, a popular, past president of Bluffton College, acted as director. I was appointed director the next year. Except for the year I spent in Winnipeg at Canadian Mennonite Bible College, I served as director for the remainder of my years at Bluffton.

My task as director of the BCSC was to contact each faculty member each year to discuss potential research projects. I assisted them to think about how nonviolence could shape their research or teaching or become visible in their disciplines. Over a period of years, my understanding of the scope and theological significance of nonviolence grew, while the program contributed to a greater awareness of nonviolence among faculty members, and eventually led to a significant faculty publication.

Elmer Neufeld retired from the presidency of Bluffton College in 1996. Our relationship was sometimes rocky during his eighteen years in office. The tension came from my development as a functioning theologian. Over time, the situation evolved and the status of the college improved. As exemplified by the president's eventual solid support of the BCSC, our last years together were good years. The following chapter deals with this situation in more detail.

16

Getting to Thanks

When Elmer Neufeld became president of Bluffton College in 1978, he inherited a difficult situation. He was president for more than half of my years in Bluffton, and for many of those years I did not make his job easier.

Early in Neufeld's presidency, the institution faced a potential decline in enrollment. Some projections showed that the number of college age students would fall twenty-five percent by 1990, resulting in closure of twenty-five percent of small colleges.

In faculty retreat in August 1976, at the beginning of my second year in Bluffton, President Benjamin Sprunger had presented a thirty-six-page manifesto with his solution to this potential decline in enrollment. Bluffton College would be re-branded as "The Christian College of Western Ohio," which meant imprinting the school with an Evangelical, that is, conservative theological identity. Bluffton College was affiliated with the General Conference Mennonite Church, the second largest of the Mennonite denominations, and had a progressive-leaning identity. Faculty, including me, rebelled against the suggested new brand. Tense discussions and stormy faculty meetings ensued, and President Sprunger resigned in April 1977. Elmer Neufeld, the dean who had hired me two years earlier, assumed the presidency early in 1978.

Neufeld was well known in the Mennonite constituency from his previous years of leadership of Mennonite Central Committee, the relief and service agency of Mennonite

138

churches. Personally, he was sympathetic with the previous president's agenda but also recognized that faculty objected. It was reported that a conservative element of the church constituency said that their future financial support of the college depended upon finding a president exactly like the one who had resigned. Neufeld reportedly told the search committee that he could be that president but without alienating the faculty. He was embracing a difficult task.

Neufeld knew that my department, the Religion Department, would come under close scrutiny. He knew my progressive outlook, but he wanted to bring me along in his move to appeal to the conservative constituency. Neufeld invited me to his office, on the second floor of College Hall, the oldest building on campus. He greeted me at the door. He stood six feet one inch tall, salt-and-pepper hair flat to his head, square jaw, lean frame, clad in gray suit and tie. We shook hands and he pointed to a captain's chair and took another for a friendly, face-to-face chat.

After the usual small talk, he got to his agenda for this conversation. "Can't we be evangelical, with a small *e*, in the true sense of the word?" he asked. Evangelical with a capital E meant the conservative identity and agenda advocated by the previous president. Spelled with a small e, however, the word turned into an adjective that meant willing to proclaim whatever one believed. Use of the term with small e would then accommodate my agenda right along with the conservative agenda. If I acquiesced to the president's desire, he could speak Evangelical language in the constituency and imply that the campus, particularly my department, went along with being evangelical.

My answer was a noncommittal, "Yes, I suppose." Actually, I resisted. I was uncomfortable implying that I was something that I was not, and in any case the real story would be easily revealed. The president also invited me to attend his more Evangelical or conservative Mennonite congregation in nearby Lima. I declined. Instead, I chose to attend First Mennonite in Bluffton, the large progressive Mennonite congregation where many of my faculty colleagues attended.

The national denominational context contributed to our uneasy relationship. Bluffton College was affiliated with the General Conference Mennonite Church. I had grown up in the Mennonite Church, the largest of the Mennonite denominations, and I graduated from its school, Goshen College. Goshen published the internationally known periodical *Mennonite Quarterly Review*, and considered itself the premier Mennonite school. A history of tension as well as cooperation existed between the two denominations and these colleges. Goshen College had a higher Mennonite profile than Bluffton, and both sides considered my relocation to Bluffton remarkable. Some Goshen colleagues asked if Bluffton was a Mennonite school, while others even asked where it was located.

I brought some of the Goshen attitude with me to Bluffton, and it did cause tension. I did not hold Goshen up as a model by name. However, when the president would talk about the need to play down Bluffton's Mennonite identity, I would advocate raising the Mennonite profile of Bluffton College. In response, President Neufeld would remind me that this was not Goshen. When I spoke in faculty meeting about raising our academic profile, the president might reply that Goshen could stress high academics, but Bluffton College had a different mission.

In my first years at Bluffton, I published articles that described the new perspectives on Anabaptist history and a historical view of the Bible in the two main Mennonite denominational periodicals. These publications gave the college visibility in the wider church. My participation in academic conferences and articles in *Mennonite Quarterly Review*, raised awareness of Bluffton in the wider Mennonite academic network. President Neufeld did recognize the value of this visibility, even as it made him nervous.

My classroom performance also caused some problems for the president. Students reported at home what I had said in class, some with approval and others appalled. When the president would complain to me, I assumed that he had received a note from an irate parent or pastor who objected to what the students reported. I did not envy President Neufeld in his struggle to maintain the financial integrity of the institution. The financial threat that he faced daily did worry me—I was a part of the school he fought for, but I could not alter my theological views.

These elements set the context for the uneasy alliance the president and I lived in for a number of years, both needing and frustrating each other. It produces a kaleidoscope of memories. The president stood by me through the controversy with Ted VanderEnde and brought in the denominational leadership to control the situation, as described in an earlier chapter. He gave me Bluffton faculty development money to pay my expenses for a trip to Goshen to do research for my C. Henry Smith Peace lecture. We had more than one conversation on how Eastern District pastors were complaining about my biblical interpretation, such as saying the book of Jonah was not a fish story but a parable about the history of Israel. When I worried about tenure, he assured me that I was wanted.

While I was working to write theology that reflected a specifically Mennonite or peace church identity, Elmer Neufeld argued that we needed to get beyond Mennonite, and he resisted stressing a Mennonite identity for Bluffton College. He definitely saw the good publicity that accrued to Bluffton College through the successful Mennonite Experience in America conference in August 1987. After resisting the mention for many years, eventually he included a statement in his annual "state of the college address" that one of the three pillars of a college was research and publication. After his initial reluctance, Neufeld came to support the Bluffton College Study Center, created in 1987, and my role as director.

Since presidents do not like to be surprised, one day I dropped by his office without an appointment to tell him a major article I had written on atonement had been accepted by *Modern Theology*. This article was my first significant publication outside of the Mennonite orbit, and I was proud of the accomplishment. But without knowing the content of the article, he warned me that if I did not stop publishing such radical pieces, even as a tenured faculty member I could still be terminated. Hesitantly, I offered that I would be interested in his response to this new statement. Almost immediately he apologized and said that he had not really meant the comment about exclusion.

Another incident that he tolerated was the story described in another chapter, of my experience at Normal '89, when I en-

dured a public attack by prominent Evangelical Ron Sider, and
Tim Epp, pastor of the large conservative, Mennonite congregation at Berne, Indiana. At one point, a member of the board of
trustees of Bluffton College told me that whenever I published
something, Neufeld was worried that folks in Berne would be
upset, not particularly a surprise since at that time the college received numbers of students and significant financial support
from Berne. At a later time Neufeld threatened that I could still
be fired if I did not accept the ontological Christology that was a
factor in the session at Normal '89. I presume that the fracas at
Normal '89 contributed to his enthusiastic support not long after
when I requested permission to accept the invitation to move to
Winnipeg, Manitoba, and Canadian Mennonite Bible College for
the 1990-91 year.

A movement in the wider church brought a significant improvement in our relationship. In 1983, the Mennonite Church
and the General Conference Mennonite Church began a merger
process that culminated in 2001. Along the way, one point of discussion was the relationship of the five Mennonite colleges to the
new denomination. Before the merger, ground rules were established for recruitment of students. A school from one Mennonite
denomination could not recruit among members of the other denomination unless a prospective student first made an inquiry.

After the merger, any school could recruit any Mennonite
student. Since Ohio had a large Mennonite Church population
that previously was off limits to Bluffton College, the change
would benefit Bluffton, provided the institution emphasized a
Mennonite profile. Access to these students would ease the president's worry about the congregation in Berne, Indiana. My activities that had previously created tension with the president
now became valuable. In June 1992, when Bluffton College was
asked to host a conference on higher education as part of the
merger process of the two denominations, my contacts in the
wider Mennonite academic network became a resource for the
president, who consulted me about the academic people that I
knew.

President Neufeld retired in 1996. In late summer of 2001
my book *The Nonviolent Atonement* appeared. It was an unam-

biguous rejection of the received, dominant, satisfaction atonement image considered orthodoxy by fundamentalists and Evangelicals, along with my suggestion for an alternative atonement image. (Following chapters expand on the story of this book.) If it had appeared fifteen years earlier, this book and the response to it in elements of the constituency would have caused President Neufeld an enormous headache.

After his retirement, he had access to a small office on the edge of campus. Occasionally I met him when he came to check his mail in Marbeck Center, the student union building. One day in late fall, a couple years after *The Nonviolent Atonement* appeared, our paths crossed in Klassen Plaza, outside of Marbeck Center. As students streamed around us, he stopped me. He had aged, his close-lying hair now mostly gray. Relaxed in retirement, he wore blue jeans and a comfortable sweater. "I want you to know," he said, "that I have recommended *The Nonviolent Atonement* to several people, and I have mentioned it a number of times in my Sunday school class." It was his Sunday school class at the congregation that years earlier I had opted not to attend. "I defended you," he continued, "I understand better now than I used to what you are about." After the tension of our early years together, this unqualified affirmation overwhelmed me. All I could say was a warm "Thank you."

17

Shifting Worldview

I read James Cone's book *God of the Oppressed* in May 1993, and it gave me a jolt. In fact, I re-read the relevant pages several times, asking myself if I had really understood what I was reading.

By this point, at what turned out to be three years into the second half of my career and some three years after my return from Winnipeg with my new identity as theologian, I was working quite specifically to inhabit this still seemingly new identity. I was producing theology far removed from my graduate work in the Reformation. I had participated in the Christology conference at Normal '89, and I published the article on "Atonement for the Nonconstantinian Church" in *Modern Theology*. I had identified the image of Christus Victor as the basis of atonement for the peace church, and I was working on an extended article for *Mennonite Quarterly Review* that would state that conclusion.

A short review and summary of the theological context in which I was working will set up the full impact of reading Cone's *God of the Oppressed*. In the Mennonite tradition in which I grew up, we had a sense of being a distinct Christian tradition, a bit outside of so-called mainstream Protestant denominations. An important part of that distinct identity was the commitment to nonviolence based on the life of Jesus. My intent was to produce theology that would reflect our distinct peace tradition. I focused on Christology, the way the church has identified Jesus, and atonement, the understanding of how the church has understood that the death of Jesus saves sinners.

As I wrote for the conference at Normal '89, in the words of the classic formula from the Council of Chalcedon (451 CE), the standard way of identifying Jesus was to say that he is "fully human and fully divine." In my analysis, I argued that making the abstract concepts of humanity and deity the foundation of faith allowed Christians to resort to the sword while professing faith in Jesus who rejected the sword. For Mennonites, I concluded that we should identify Jesus by starting with the story of his life, because that is where we find his rejection of the sword.

The satisfaction image, which is the standard, dominant view of atonement, said that God sent Jesus to die for the sins of humankind. In my analysis, I argued that this image needed only Jesus' death and ignored his life and resurrection, and it pictured Jesus as submitting willingly to unjust violence because his Father willed it. This was an unhealthy image for a tradition that emphasized using the life of Jesus as a model. As an alternative, I said that the work of Jesus came from studying his life of confronting evil, with a culmination in resurrection as victory over the powers of evil.

This approach reflected one of the lesser known historical atonement images, called Christus Victor, which is Latin for the victorious Christ. After identifying the symbols in Revelation with the church's confrontation of the powers of evil represented by Roman empire, with victory in Jesus' resurrection, I recognized that Revelation had a multifaceted version of Christus Victor, which stood as a complement to the image in the Gospels. Since this church in Revelation predates the church that made peace with the sword, this atonement image is particularly appropriate for the peace church. I wrote several articles for Mennonites that suggested a version of Christus Victor as the appropriate atonement image for the peace church.

With the sense of having an answer for Mennonites in hand, out of curiosity I wondered what some other distinct tradition outside of the mainstream might have to say on these issues. I knew only that Black theology existed along with one name, that of James Cone, whose book *Black Theology and Black Power* I had read in seminary more than two decades earlier. I had yet to learn how well known he was as the founder of the Black Theology Movement. I went to the Bluffton College library. I ran my finger down the row of books by James Cone, and virtually at random I put my finger on *God of the Oppressed* and pulled it off the shelf.

What I read overwhelmed me. Cone made the same critique of "fully human and fully divine" that I did, except that where I said these abstract categories accommodated the sword, Cone said that they accommodated slavery and racism. His answer was to focus on the story of Jesus, interpreted as liberator of the oppressed. Cone's critique of standard atonement was parallel to mine except that Cone said that the image of Jesus submitting to unjust violence because his father willed it modeled slaves submitting to beatings by slave masters because the master willed it. And like my answer, Cone's answer to atonement was also Christus Victor with focus on the life of Jesus and resurrection.

When I read these comments by Cone, I had a hard time believing that I, a junior theologian little known outside the Mennonite world, had made observations on the history of doctrine parallel to observations by the renowned James Cone. Eventually, I decided I had to verify these observations with James Cone himself. I regularly attended the annual meeting of the American Academy of Religion, which met the weekend before Thanksgiving in a large American city. With perhaps 6,000 scholars in attendance, it provided multiple opportunities for meeting people and networking. By scoping out the sessions on Black theology, I hoped to find James Cone.

At AAR in Washington, D.C., on 22 November 1993, I succeeded in identifying James Cone sitting a couple rows ahead of me in a session on Black theology. On the back of my business card, I wrote that I wanted to ask him a question and passed it up to him. He turned, we made eye contact, and he pointed to the exit. I followed him out into a busy corridor. Conversations surrounded us, and people hurried along, looking for their particular sessions.

Cone said, "I want to hear the next paper. I will give you five minutes." Quickly I explained my observations that seemed parallel to his, and I asked if my observations were valid. "Of course they are valid," he said, "but you aren't saying anything that we in the black community don't already know." As a young theologian hoping to find a new and publishable idea that might fly with the folks who attended AAR, my spirit sagged. "Since you have already made this critique of standard theology," I offered, "perhaps there is nothing left for me to write." Cone looked down at my name badge. He said, "Oh, no, Professor Weaver. You are one of the few white folks who knows. You go tell the white folks."

That conversation changed my worldview. Until that moment, I thought that I was writing a theology for my small circle of Mennonites. But with Cone's affirmation of my observations and his encouragement to publish, it took only a few moments of reflection to realize that I was actually involved with theologians like Cone in a major challenge to the entire edifice of inherited standard theology. In short, I was addressing the entire Christian tradition. Alongside dealing with issues of the sword and direct violence for the peace church, I needed to include and deal with issues of social justice such as racism. The more I thought about it, the wider my horizon of theologizing became. As far as my long connection with the Mennonite tradition was concerned, I hoped that that community would also notice my work and recognize that they were included as an important part of my audience.

In terms of the chess metaphor, developing an atonement image that incorporated my learning from James Cone was definitely an important new move. At the same time, beyond the chess metaphor, I was also experiencing theology as a cooperative endeavor, with mutual support and learning from allies Cone and others, and with growing awareness of the context from which theology emerges as well as its wider purpose and audience.

I made additional contacts with Cone. We chatted at the annual meetings of AAR. I got permission from my administration to invite him to speak at Bluffton College. He accepted the invitation.

In 2001 my book *The Nonviolent Atonement* was published by Eerdmans, a major publisher of theological writing. It contains a chapter on Black theology, in which the writing of James

Cone has a prominent place. That year, at the annual meeting of AAR/SBL, a friend and I went to a session in which Cone was to be honored for his lifetime of work. We walked down in front and grabbed seats in the front row. James Cone came up the aisle and passed in front of us on his way to the stage. As he passed, we greeted each other. He took another step and turned back to me. "You wrote a good book," he said. I realized that I now fully inhabited my identity as a theologian.

18

Theological Surprises

Studying Black theology drew me into feminist and womanist theologies, two schools of thought that also challenged the received tradition. Learning from feminist and womanist theologians proved a stimulating educational experience, with learning in unusual spaces and surprising ways.

I picked up an important concept in feminist understandings of atonement theology when my colleague Betty Sommer, a professor of social work and an ardent advocate of women's rights, suggested sometime in the early 1990s that our Sunday school class at First Mennonite church read *Christianity, Patriarchy and Abuse*. We agreed.

The first chapter offered a sharp critique of Anselm's view of atonement. The authors, Joanne Carlson Brown and Rebecca Parker, suggested that when "God the Father" sends "Jesus the innocent Son" to die for the sins of humankind, it is an image of "divine child abuse." A following chapter by Rita Nakashima Brock offered another version of the same image. These feminist writers argued that this image is dangerous for women, who are encouraged to submit to abusive husbands or fathers in the way that Jesus submitted to abuse because his father, the God the Father of classic Trinity, willed it.

The Sunday school class met in the small, concrete block building next to the church. We were perhaps fifteen people, a mixture of professors and other professions, sitting in a circle on metal folding chairs. Betty asked what I thought about the notion of divine child abuse. After a brief moment of reflection, I said, "It makes sense to me."

I promptly added this feminist critique and the phrase "divine child abuse" to my ongoing development of ways to critique the standard satisfaction imagery, along with the names of Rebecca Parker, President of Starr King School of Ministry, and Rita Nakishima Brock, then a theology professor at Pacific Lutheran University. At the time, I had no idea that Brock and Parker would become a writing team and two of the most important voices in feminist atonement theology, nor did it occur to me to see myself as their colleague. In the moment, I knew only that their feminist critique and the image of divine child abuse fit well with what I had earlier learned from Black theology about the way satisfaction atonement modeled slavery and abuse.

My education in theology written by women was not limited to learning from books. In November 1993, I arrived at the annual meeting of American Academy of Religion in Washington, D.C., ready to expand my newly stimulated interest in feminist theology. In the thick program book, I observed sessions on both feminist and womanist theology. *Interesting*, I mused, *I would think that feminist and womanists were synonyms*. I wondered why a synonym was necessary.

To find out, I went to a session with the "synonym" *womanist* in the title. As I often did, I strolled down the center aisle and found a seat in the front row. Once I had settled myself and had my notebook out and pen ready to take notes, I looked up at the panel of participants seated behind a long table at the front of the room a few feet away from me. The panel consisted of six African-American women. I turned around and looked back at the audience. What I saw was a sea of Black faces, all of whom seemed to be looking right at me. Clearly I had wandered onto foreign turf. Thus did I stumble into the fact that womanist theology was theology written by Black women. As I was about to find out, it was different from feminist theology. Early womanists endorsed a three-fold agenda focused on dealing with the white orientation of early feminist theology, the male dominance of the Black church, and poverty.

The womanist session intrigued me. Alongside Black theology and feminist theology, this was another example of a group that was excluded by the mainstream that purported to speak for everyone. I sensed the importance of the moment for the participants, and I was quite aware that I needed to respect their ownership of the meeting. At the conclusion of the session, cautiously I approached the speaker whose observations seemed most compatible with my concerns. She sat on the right end of the long speakers table. I posed the same question that I had earlier to James Cone, whether my critique of the received tradition was a parallel to her critique, and I received a similar answer. My world and worldview were expanding rapidly.

These African-American women were quite conscious that they were opening a new frontier in theology, and it was important to recognize their domain. I attended other womanist sessions, but I sat on the edge as a way to acknowledge their territory. I recall a particular session, with perhaps twenty women in the audience, and I was sitting up against the right wall, facing the speakers. I heard four papers, which stimulated a question.

Finally, after considerable hesitancy, in the period for open discussion I raised my hand. When the chair recognized me, I acknowledged that it was their session but wondered if I could ask a question. "Of course," the chair responded. "Go ahead, we'll help you." I stood to pose my question, which concerned implications of the presentations that I had just heard. As I sat down, the chair said, "And you thought you would have trouble asking a question." The panelists took my question seriously, and welcomed me into their discussion. I was learning a lot, both about theology but also about respecting an arena that was not my own, and how to enter discussions that were outside of my comfort zone.

Eventually, I would learn an important parallel to divine child abuse in womanist thought. In her book *Sisters in the Wilderness*, Delores Williams, prominent womanist theologian, wrote that to accept Jesus' submission to unjust suffering and violence as the basis of forgiveness of sin because God the Father willed it was to make Jesus the "ultimate surrogate figure," who validated all the unjust surrogacy foisted on Black women throughout history. Williams was referring to the many ways in which Black women have been forced to fulfill roles that belonged to other people, such as serving as sexual surrogates for white women whose husbands forced themselves on slaves, or caring for white children in the master's house rather than their own children, or earning a living for a family after the man of the house had been run off from fear of lynching.

Womanist theology provided an important, additional contribution to my critique of the satisfaction imagery, and impetus to my ongoing assertion of a new atonement image. However, others were not as intrigued by womanists as I was. An example was the prominent pacifist ethicist with whom I sometimes checked ideas. As we stood in the middle of a bustling lobby at an AAR meeting, I told him about my learning from womanists for my atonement argument and asked for his opinion. His answer surprised me. He said, "Go slow with womanists. They might turn out to be a fad. You wouldn't want to be caught writing about a fad."

Despite the warning, I included a chapter on womanist theology in my book *The Nonviolent Atonement*. This conversation did serve as a reminder that not everyone committed to nonviolence followed my ongoing critique of the classic tradition that I believed accommodated the sword. Meanwhile, womanist theology had staying power and remains in conversation with other theological orientations.

Through such experiences I accumulated a store of theological learning rare for a white man, as illustrated by the fact that in AAR sessions on Black or womanist theology, few other attenders looked like me. This learning came to fruition a few years later in my book, *The Nonviolent Atonement*, whose first edition appeared in 2001. When I experienced pushback from both Mennonites and those in other denominations committed to the classic standard atonement tradition, it was thrilling and gratifying to be part of a wider movement that challenged the standard tradition. Finding common cause with those that had experienced racial discrimination was especially satisfying.

The Nonviolent Atonement appeared amid a flourishing era of Bluffton College with an administration that contributed to its arrival. The following chapter exemplifies this era.

19

The Golden Age

During my last ten years at Bluffton, one third of my teaching career, I participated in one of the best eras in the history of the college. On occasion I called it a Golden Age. I pursued a busy schedule, with activities both on and off campus, continuing theological learning and development on several fronts, along with theological challenges to confront.

One essential element of this era was the administration of Lee Snyder, who took office as president of Bluffton College on 1 August 1996. She had previously served as dean at Eastern Mennonite University. When President Snyder assumed office, the college was in a good place. Enrollment had been increasing, and the financial worries of the previous decade had eased. The unaware might be deceived by the president's stature—barely five feet—and pleasant demeanor. She was a decisive leader, who knew how to make things happen for her institution. Her presidency constituted a historic moment for Bluffton. She was the first woman to serve as president of a Mennonite college and Bluffton College was the beneficiary. I was immensely proud to have had the privilege to serve on the search committee that selected Lee Snyder as president.

President Snyder hired John Kampen as Dean of Academic Affairs. Kampen was a scholar who specialized in the Dead Sea Scrolls. He was serving as dean at Payne Theological Seminary when President Snyder called him to Bluffton. Both Snyder and Kampen supported research by faculty members, and unleashed a great deal of pent up, creative, academic energy that animated the decade. Dean Kampen gave me good advice when I applied to the Louisville Foundation for the grant that supported the writing of *The Nonviolent Atonement*. President Snyder guided me through the controversy that accompanied the announcement of the grant.

Gerald Mast joined the Bluffton College faculty in the Communication Department in fall 1996. After the invitation for me to speak at Pittsburgh Mennonite Church that Gerald had arranged in January 1993, we had chatted at a couple conferences. I was delighted when he interviewed at Bluffton in April 1996. Later, Gerald had to remind me that what would become a twenty-five-year-long, mutually enriching cooperation, actually began during his interview. At the reception where he met faculty members, I slipped him a printout of a manuscript I was working on and asked for his comments. Once installed at Bluffton, Gerald's office was located in the floor below mine, which made frequent conversation a sustained reality.

From Gerald I learned that I was "postmodern," but I had no idea what that meant. Stated most briefly, according to many scholars, "modernity" described the idea, inherited from the Enlightenment, that reason could establish a universal truth accessible to all people everywhere, if we searched long enough. The condition of "postmodernity," then, was the recognition that every statement of truth reflected a particular context and no universal reference point for truth could be established for all people everywhere. For me, that meant that my effort to develop theology that reflected an Anabaptist, peace-church perspective was actually a postmodern search.

From me, Gerald learned to see the standard formulas of Christology and Trinity—Nicea's statement that Jesus is "one in being with the Father," Chalcedon's "truly God and truly Man," and the Cappadocian Fathers' trinitarian formula of "one God in Three Persons"—were not transcendently true. They were not unquestioned givens but rather particular statements that answered specific questions and reflected a particular context and worldview. In their context they were not false. But in a different context, one could develop theology without being beholden to them. Thus Gerald supported my efforts to develop theology for

Anabaptists. As earlier touched on, I had been engaged in an extended conversation with A. James Reimer, theology professor at Conrad Grebel University College, who argued that theology for Mennonites should rest on and begin with the Nicene Creed. Hence the discussion about postmodernity and contextualism was enriching for both Gerald and me.

One faculty initiative supported by the administration of Lee Snyder and John Kampen was the organization of academic conferences. Gerald Mast and his then-wife Sue Biesecker, both professors in the Communication Department, proposed a major conference on Anabaptists and postmodernity. It met in August 1998 with more than one hundred registrants. We invited John Howard Yoder as keynote speaker.

After Yoder's untimely death in December 1997, Stanley Hauerwas, well-known pacifist ethicist and professor from Duke University, gave the keynote address. In the discussion period, Hauerwas was asked about the Weaver-Reimer argument on Christology. He replied that it was a crucial discussion but that he supported Reimer's side. This comment was at least a second awareness that while Hauerwas shared my commitment to nonviolence, he considered Nicene Christology normative and rejected my project to develop theology that reflected the peace church. For this conference I contributed a presentation on womanist theology and how its particularity pointed to the particular context of Nicene Christology and thus opened the door to an understanding of Christology that fit the peace church.

At the conference in Bluffton occurred one of the series of conversations I had with Mennonite theologian Tom Finger, who had a distinct, hybrid approach to a theology for Mennonites. As I describe it in one sentence, Finger kept the classic, assumed orthodox language of Nicea, Chalcedon, and the Trinity, but then filled that framework with individual pieces picked from various locations—liberal, evangelical, Anabaptist, or Mennonite—depending on the audience. In this way, Finger claimed that his theology was both Catholic and Mennonite, or orthodox and Anabaptist. The unchanging point, however, was the retention of the classic foundation. In my analysis, when

Finger picked individual pieces from various theologies, he did not fully recognize that these small pieces were not stand-alone items but rather fit within and reflected a larger context. Further, his revised orthodox theology was no longer the orthodoxy that he claimed to have retained.

Tom Finger and I had engaged in a number of previous exchanges. Finger had written a response to my presentation at Normal '89, which appeared in the published record of that event. We had debated at several conferences and in print as well. I wrote an extended critique of the methodology in Finger's massive 2004 book, *A Contemporary Anabaptist Theology*. My critique appeared in an issue of the periodical *Direction*, with reply in the following issue. I also wrote a response to Finger in the volume edited by Sanders, *Atonement and Violence*, and in the revised edition of *The Nonviolent Atonement*.

Earlier in this memoir I described how the personal stories of James Reimer and myself were reflected in our approaches to theology. A discussion at an AAR session similarly illustrated Finger's approach. In a session he had sketched his faith autobiography—growing up without any religious identity, then coming to faith with Evangelicals, and finally adopting pacifism after reading writings of John Howard Yoder. In the question-and-answer period, I suggested that Finger's theology reflected an American multicultural background—taking pieces from various traditions and then fitting them into a mosaic. Finger replied, "Not mosaic but synthesis." As was the case with Reimer, I could appreciate where Finger came from, even as I did not follow his results.

Some theological challenges were debated at the Anabaptist Seminar that met every two years for scholars in the Midwest. A particular issue of contention was the contextual character of theology and sixteenth-century Anabaptist references to the classic creedal statements. The debate had several facets. Historian C. Arnold Snyder argued that the essence of Anabaptism was determined by what all Anabaptists had in common. He described a core of beliefs that characterized all Anabaptists. Since Anabaptists referred to the classic creeds and the Trinity, the core included adherence to classic orthodoxy as an Anabaptist characteristic. Since not all Anabaptists were pacifists, pacifism was no longer included as a core Anabaptist attribute. The historians argued that they depended on sources, on documents, and this conclusion was what they read in the sources.

In our conversation, Gerald and I agreed that this idea of a common core reduced Anabaptism to a pale version of the mass church that they had rejected. Our view was that Anabaptism constituted a distinct tradition that existed in its own right. We addressed the historical arguments in several meetings of the Anabaptist Seminar: one at Goshen College in April 1999, and another in Goshen in April 2001, when we took along two of our students.

Using rhetorical analysis, Gerald argued that what Anabaptists disputed was as important as what they agreed on. Further, Anabaptists were the only group in the Reformation that debated about use of the sword, and from these debates, it was those who rejected the sword that emerged to carry the designation Anabaptist. Thus Anabaptism should be recognized as the origin of Mennonites as a peace church.

I used theological analysis to examine the context in which Anabaptists used the classic creedal language. My argument was that they revised or rejected the classic language in ways that reflected their new view of the church that had rejected the mass church. I used the celestial flesh Christology of Menno Simons as an example. When judged by Chalcedonian terminology, Menno was an embarrassment, a poor theologian, if not actually heretical. But if Menno is evaluated as an Anabaptist who rejected the mass church, he could and should receive credit for the initiative of attempting to develop a Christology that reflected his commitment to Jesus' rejection of violence and to a church that rejected the sword. Some years later I made a parallel argument for Pilgram Marpeck. In addition, the revised edition of *Becoming Anabaptist* published in 2005 also contains an appendix that responded to the idea of defining Anabaptism in terms of this common core.

Following the seminar in 2001, we took our students to a cafe on Main Street in Goshen to debrief the session. As we sipped coffee and munched on pastries, we replayed some comments. One memorable comment followed my argument that a theology for Anabaptists could develop without dependence on the Nicene Creed. In response, a grad student with the contingent from Conrad Grebel College had burst out, "But without the Nicene Creed, how would we know what to believe?" In the cafe, our mood was jocular. The students laughed at the idea that for three centuries until Nicea came along, Christians were left with no idea what to believe, or that without Nicea today we would not know how to read the Bible. Gerald and I came away convinced that our arguments made sense and had withstood all challenges.

Our ongoing response to the view that challenged Anabaptism as the origin of the contemporary peace church was papers we presented to the Anabaptist Seminar at Eastern Mennonite University in April 2006. Gerald presented a paper focused on the sixteenth century, and I wrote about a contemporary Anabaptist identity. Our intent was to present a new paradigm of Anabaptism as a multifaceted movement of a socially engaged church that returned continually to the narrative of Jesus as a foundation. This view could encompass the several different Anabaptist movements in the sixteenth century, while retaining rejection of violence as an integral element, even if not all adherents practiced nonviolence. These two presentations were expanded to become our first co-authored book, *Defenseless Christianity: Anabaptism for a Nonviolent Church* that appeared in 2009 with the main title borrowed from the long title of *Martyrs Mirror*.

As the calendar moved toward the turn to the second millennium, Loren Johns, Bluffton professor of New Testament, took the lead in organizing a conference on millennialism that met in August 1999. Paul Boyer, professor of American history at the University of Wisconsin-Madison, gave a keynote address on the history of millennialism in the United States. For this conference, I wrote a paper on the historical antecedents of the images in the book of Revelation and its implications for my atonement discussions. Data from this paper as well as the paper for the postmodernism conference tested arguments that later appeared in my book *The Nonviolent Atonement*.

Another initiative was the inauguration of a new book series, co-sponsored by Bluffton College and the Mennonite Historical Society at Goshen College. It was called the C. Henry Smith Series after the professor of that name who taught history at Bluffton College from 1913 to 1948. The series was designed to deal with issues in contemporary Anabaptist and Mennonite studies, as a parallel to the history series, Studies in Anabaptist and Mennonite History, published at Goshen College. I was named the first editor of the C. Henry Smith series, a position I held until 2020.

A collection of edited presentations from the postmodernity conference became *Anabaptists and Postmodernity*, the first volume in the C. Henry Smith series, a fitting beginning to a series begun in the first year with the date 2000, even if it was technically the last year of the previous millennium. Gerald and Sue served as the editors of the volume, but I was enlisted to deal with some troublesome contributions. In particular, two essays that we wanted to use came to the editors in poor shape—lacking references, full of sentence fragments, and barely coherent. Gerald and I worked together to bring these two chapters into publishable form. This effort foreshadowed more such editing efforts.

My book *Anabaptist Theology in Face of Postmodernity* became the second volume in the C. Henry Smith series in 2000. This book contained a statement on how doing theology differed between the United States and Canada, as well as early versions of my analysis of several centuries of Anabaptist and Mennonite theological writings on atonement theology. This small book had surprising staying power, as exemplified by a Facebook post in 2020 that recommended the book because it demonstrated what happened to Anabaptist theology that got too close to Fundamentalism.

In February 2000, during the sabbatical leave in which *The Nonviolent Atonement* was written (see following chapter), I visited my daughter Sonia and her husband Alain Epp Weaver and their two children in Gaza, where they served with Mennonite Central Committee. One evening, Alain and Sonia took me for a meal with a family in a Palestinian refugee camp. I will call the couple Ahmed and Fatima. While the term *camp* brings up images of tents, these camps for Palestinian refugees are actually small towns of concrete houses, some unfinished. As we walked along streets narrow enough to extend our arms and touch the houses on either side, my daughter reminded me that Gaza has the highest population density in the world. That fact means that the average room occupancy would be seven or eight people, with some much more crowded. Ahmed and Fatima and four children were relatively well off with four rooms—kitchen, living-dining room, two sleeping rooms—with furniture, and cooking equipment.

I was glad to observe the setting and I enjoyed the meal immensely. We sat in traditional Palestinian fashion, on cushions arrayed around the floor and walls of the dining room. The food arrived on two large platters, placed in the center of the room, heaped high with *maklube*—a delicious mixture of rice, potatoes, chicken, eggplant, and cauliflower. We ate the maklube with tablespoons from these platters. Before each diner were placed bowls of yogurt, a vegetable condiment, and a beef broth, in which to dip the rice. The maklube was followed by peanuts in the shell and roasted watermelon seeds, accompanied by sweet, hot tea. The meal concluded with tiny cups of hot, sweet coffee, and *kanafi*, a fantastic dessert of baked cheese and honey. It was a sumptuous and memorable meal.

The setting fostered conversation. During and after the meal we talked about anything and everything. Ahmed spoke excellent English, and translated everything that Fatima said. One topic concerned the Taliban, who at that pre-September 11 time still ruled Afghanistan. Ahmed was adamant: "The Taliban is *not* Islam."

I asked about Islam and the role of women. Fatima spoke lovingly about the freedom she felt as a Muslim woman. "I can do anything I want," she said. "Islam teaches the equality of men and women." "Yes," Ahmed added, "the idea that Islam teaches women to stay home and not become educated is *not true Islam*." Ahmed went on to talk about the pride he felt for Fatima. Although the occupation of Gaza prevented its actualization, he could proclaim, "She can drive, she can study and pursue a profession." "Islam is God's gift to women," Fatima concluded. I was impressed.

In the car with Sonia and Alain on the way back to their apartment in Gaza City, I pursued the topic of women in Islam. Drawing on my alleged knowledge as a professor of theology, I said, "What Fatima said about Islam was impressive." Then with the seemingly inevitable qualifier, I added, "But, there is still the matter of 'headship.'"

"Da-ad," my daughter said, with the two-syllable emphasis that indicated I was in trouble, "Did you hear Fatima or Ahmed say anything about headship?" I had to admit that I had not.

I was surprised at my ignorance, about how much I had assumed, and how I had read the idea of headship from Christian Evangelicalism into what I was hearing. I was doubly surprised to learn that both Fatima and Ahmed supported abortion rights. These surprises continued the learnings about Arab culture, Palestinians, and Islam that had begun with my experience in Algeria, learnings about being cautions with assumptions, and now about seeing Muslim women as individuals rather than in term of the often-stated stereotype of being oppressed by their religion. In Fatima's case, the oppressor was not Islam but the Israeli occupiers of Gaza.

As director of the Bluffton College Study Center, each year I talked with each faculty member about a potential summer research project. My particular focus was to help faculty to do projects that made nonviolence visible in their disciplines. After several years of these discussions, there was a heightened sense among faculty of the sometimes surprising ways that nonviolence could shape research or teaching in a variety of disciplines.

A specific focus for this accumulation of faculty learning about nonviolence was precipitated when at a church conference, Gerald Mast observed the Goshen College president signing autographs on a small book written by Goshen faculty and published by Goshen's in-house Pinchpenny Press. It took only a few minutes of discussion for Gerald and me to conclude that we could produce our own product, impressive in its own right, with our faculty. We developed a proposal, using essays that we had written and several that we knew about from colleagues.

We got an appointment with Dean John Kampen. In his small office, his desk faced the wall. As Gerald and I entered, he swiveled toward us and indicated that we should take the two captain's chairs across from him. He offered us cups of espresso made from the press he kept there. While he prepared the coffee and we enjoyed its aroma, he engaged us in small talk. Once we had our cups, he asked what we wanted to discuss. We explained the source and impetus for our proposal, and what we thought that we could produce.

We finished our recital and eyed his face framed by salt-and-pepper hair and a neatly trimmed beard. The dean was not one to speak quickly or rapidly. We waited. Finally, with a twinkle in his eye, he said, "You can do better than reprinting some essays. Don't cut any corners. Do it right and involve the whole faculty." He sent us next door to Assistant Dean Bob Pfeifer from whom we could secure faculty development money for the project. Gerald and I set out to produce a book that we could sell to a professional publisher.

We invited all faculty to a meeting to consider the possibility of producing a book that dealt with issues of nonviolence across the curriculum. To signal the importance of the project, we reserved a conference room at the Comfort Inn on the edge of town and ordered a catered lunch. Twenty-nine faculty attended the luncheon, and most agreed to proceed with the project. We ended up with contributions from twenty-four faculty members. The disciplines included history, political science, communication, literature, art, music, economics, criminal justice, psychology, cell biology, animal behavior, mathematics, education, and business administration, as well as the expected Bible and theology.

We enlisted Glen Stassen, well-known pacifist ethicist from Fuller Theological Seminary, to write an introductory chapter that defined the issues. Along with his research assistant Michael Westmoreland-White, the authors defined violence as "damage to a victim that overpowers the victim's consent." This definition covered not only violence with weapons, but also harmful systems and structures—systemic violence—such as racism, patriarchy, sexism, heterosexism, and poverty.

By this point in 2002, I was a senior member of the faculty. Gerald and I were a good editing team. For example, when a faculty member was uncertain about providing a chapter, Gerald told me, "You talk to her. She is afraid of you." On another instance, we agreed that a manuscript submitted was much too long for our book. We agreed on how to handle it. With Gerald firmly behind me, as the senior member of our team, it was my job to face an irate faculty member and explain why we deleted the middle third of his essay and then reversed the order of his first and third sections.

Chapters for this project also contributed much to my learning. One example came from theater education. The chapter showed the problematic dimensions of the Method, a common technique for training actors. It can include helping students to overcome inhibitions by forcing them to perform an act in public that they usually perform in private. With the power dynamic between teacher and student, along with gender differences, the Method has significant potential for violence against students. A chapter in psychology showed that college textbooks dealt with the impact of violence on individuals but ignored the impact of the violence and trauma of war, whether on the perpetrators or the recipients of that violence. Another chapter dealt with the North American Free Trade Agreement [NAFTA] that was passed in 1994 with claims that all sides would benefit. In fact, NAFTA perpetrated violence on thousands of peasant farmers in Mexico when lower priced products produced by agribusiness in the United States flooded the local markets and forced the peasant farmers out of business.

We edited the contribution of Stassen and Westmoreland-White and the faculty chapters into the manuscript that became *Teaching Peace: Nonviolence and the Liberal Arts*. This book expressed my long-held conviction that nonviolence and the rejection of violence was more than an ethical principle. It is in fact a perspective from which to view the world and engage with it. The fact that a number of faculty were already engaged in such projects strengthened my own conviction, and I was encouraged by those for whom the idea was new but eagerly joined the program.

At the annual meeting of American Academy of Religion in November 2002, I visited publishers. For a reason that we had not anticipated, it was a difficult book to sell. Many editors told me that we had an excellent idea and that it looked like a quality product. However, it had too many different disciplines to fit into their particular line of books, whether Bible or theology or ethics or religious history. We were thus very pleased to find a home for the manuscript at Rowman & Littlefield. *Teaching Peace: Nonviolence and the Liberal Arts* was published in 2003.

The publication of *Teaching Peace* led to other opportunities. One was a symposium at Baylor University in early November 2003, in which Gerald Mast, Angela Montel, and I participated. Montel was a biology professor from Bluffton College. Gerald and I read papers on topics that folks likely expected.

However, the audience really responded to Montel's presentation, in which she described the impact of violent language in cell biology. For example, the idea of killer cells in the body fighting off harmful germ invasions may lead to overuse of antibacterial products and efforts to raise children in environments with few exposures to bacteria or viruses, whereas numerous studies show that children raised around daily contact with farm animals develop hay fever and allergies less frequently than children from nonfarm families. Audience members told us it was Montel's paper that convinced them that we really took nonviolence seriously. We also traveled with several of the writers of *Teaching Peace* to Eastern Mennonite University for seminars on the book, and Gerald and I did a workshop for a regional meeting of Mennonites at Central District Conference.

In late winter of 2003, President George W. Bush led the United States to accept an invasion of Iraq. The war began on 20 March 2003. Antiwar activism filled the day. In my class on War, Peace, and Nonviolence, I carried in the *Toledo Blade* of that morning and read the headline that began "War Has Erupted." My remarks to the class concerned the seemingly universal assumption that war is "inevitable" and just happens.

Not true, I said. Planes don't fly themselves, guns don't pull their own triggers. Wars happen because somewhere, usually in an office, a leader makes a decision to "go" and gives the order to "go," and then other folks follow that order, so the planes take off and the triggers are pulled that begin the war.

Later that day I participated in two antiwar events. With several faculty colleagues and some students, I joined an antiwar demonstration at the Village Park. After some brief speeches and hymns, we held antiwar signs and formed a line that walked back and forth on the overpass across the highway. A lot of cars and semis gave honks of approval; four cars with pro-war signs circled by a number of times. That evening First Mennonite Church sponsored a peace vigil. In this service I repeated a statement similar to one that I had given earlier at the Village Park. Obviously our actions would not stop the war, I said. Nonetheless, they were important as a symbol of another way. But equally important was the fact that these actions were more than a symbol. In the performance of the symbolic acts, for a brief moment the peaceable reign of God was actually present on earth in the people assembled. That speech recalled my experience in Haiti a decade earlier when I first realized the reality dimensions of symbolic actions.

A believers church conference at Eastern Mennonite University in September 2004 provided an opportunity for me to articulate another dimension of a worldview shaped by Jesus' rejection of violence. In particular, I presented an argument that rejected the common assumption of two-kingdom theology, which has long existed in multiple versions.

For example, Martin Luther had said that the Christian was nonresistant personally, thus living in the kingdom of God. However, out of love for the neighbor, the Christian should use the sword to serve the government in the kingdom of the world, protecting the good and punishing evil.

The Anabaptist statement of the *Schleitheim Brotherly Union* says that the sword was ordained of God but outside of the perfection of Christ. As a boy, I recall knowing that nonresistant Mennonites did not go to war, but having a vague sense of being glad that there was an army that would protect us from the

communists, even though as nonresistant I would never participate in that army.

More recently, a new version was stated in terms of two
voices—in the voice that reflects the reign of God, all wars are
wrong, but in the other voice, one should be silent in seemingly
just cases such as the Gulf War of 1990 or the supposed humani-
tarian incursion into Somalia in 1993. In such cases, it was said,
wise policy analysts from places like Harvard know more about
the exigencies of foreign policy than Mennonite professors in
Midwest colleges.

In other words, traditional two-kingdom theology, as well as
any new variant, describes two ethics, one for Christians defined
by the kingdom of God and the other shaped by the world's political forces. The questions concerned how Christians fit into
these two kingdoms, with nonresistant Mennonites refusing to
bear the sword of the kingdom of the world while acquiescing to
military actions of government.

I objected to the idea that Christians who professed nonviolence would openly support violent actions in which they would
not personally participate. More importantly, I developed a theological alternative to any version of two-kingdom theology. I
agree that two entities exist, but I objected to the idea that the
"kingdom of the world" had a God-given identity andvdivinely
ordained way of acting. One entity is the reign of God, I argued,
but everything else is not the reign of God. I called it the "non-
reign-of-God." This discussion of the non-reign-of-God was
published in *Exiles in the Empire*.

Non-reign-of-God covers all institutions, persons, and
fallen creation that do not yet recognize the will of God. Calling it
non-reign-of-God makes clear that these structures are not following a God-ordained order. They are fallen forces that do not
recognize the reign of God. The forces of the non-reign-of-God
do provide a function of order in the world, and adherents to the
reign of God can of course cooperate with forces of the non-
reign-of-God when appropriate, as in programs to combat
poverty or systemic racism, or civilian patrols, and much more.

When it is a matter of resort to violence by the forces of the
non-reign-of-God, the adherents of the reign of God should not

bless that violence. Rather they should pose alternatives that
would illustrate and exemplify ways to function that would
move in the direction of the reign of God.

An example might be working in restorative justice in contrast to the usual retributive justice, or starting conversations
and posing creative alternatives to violence. I have had letters to
the editor published in our local paper *The Wisconsin State
Journal*, in which I advocated building schools and homes for
refugees in Afghanistan as more effective than military action in
combating terrorism, and suggesting that it would be cheaper to
buy North Korea's nuclear program rather than building up for
and then paying the enormous cost of a nuclear war. More recently, the paper published my letter that described the Singing
Revolution in Estonia and the Revolution of the Candles in
Leipzig, Germany, as potentially exemplifying alternatives to
war in Ukraine.

It is gratifying to see these various suggestions in print, and
to have a few people thank me for these letters. While these letters in the paper do not materially change the situation, I count
it a success when a small statement keeps in view the fact that violence and war are not inevitable.

A major initiative by the Bluffton administration was the
application for a grant of two million dollars from the Lilly
Foundation. The grant's overall theme was to foster the peace
church identity and mission of Bluffton College, with a particular focus on anti-racism. The grant supported multiple programs, several of which intersected with my projects. For one, as
a followup to our publication of *Teaching Peace*, the grant had
money to sponsor a major conference on "nonviolence across
the curriculum." The conference met in May 2004 with 175 registrants from fifty colleges. A keynote address by Susan Brooks
Thistlethwaite, professor of theology and president of Chicago
Theological Seminary, received a standing ovation. This conference brought Bluffton College a wealth of good publicity.

Another component of the grant from the Lilly Foundation
was significant money for guest speakers. I was put in charge of
inviting these speakers, along with being named director of the
weekly forum series. These roles were added to my role as direc-

tor of the Study Center. Together these roles became a third-time position, with a clerical assistant.

The role of Forum Director enabled me to host a number of impressive speakers. There was Gwynne Dyer, Canadian journalist, who had written *War: the Lethal Custom*. A particularly relevant speaker was James Loewen, author of *Lies My Teacher Told Me*, whose primary focus in his address was on the way that slavery and racism have been eliminated from discussions of United States history. Another speaker of note was Alan Page, a member of the professional football Hall of Fame following a fifteen-year career with the Minnesota Vikings and Chicago Bears, and later a Supreme Court Justice for the state of Minnesota. In his address, Page emphasized the importance of education, telling the audience that learning to study, going to law school, and becoming a Supreme Court justice was much more significant than anything he did as a football player.

Another important guest speaker was Daniel Boyarin, an Orthodox Jewish scholar from the University of California, Berkeley. Boyarin's book *Border Lines,* presents an approach to the Jewish-Christian schism parallel to John Howard Yoder's argument in *Jewish-Christian Schism Revisited*. The two authors point to the fact that in the early centuries there were both Jewish and Christian groups that worshipped together although they disagreed on whether Jesus was the Messiah. Since scholars have never agreed on the date when the schism became permanent, both Boyarin and Yoder implied that we could still be having that discussion as a kind of in-house argument. That is, rather than seeing Judaism and Christianity as mutually exclusive religions, we should see their relationship as a conversation between different factions within one group.

I was able to use contacts developed in the academic network to invite several prominent writers of black and womanist theology. One was James Cone, author of many books on black theology, whose extemporaneous banter with students in defending an anti-racism agenda was a highlight.

I invited the married couple of Karen Baker-Fletcher, theology professor at Perkins School of Theology at Southern Methodist University and Garth Kasimu Baker-Fletcher, one-time theology professor at Claremont School of Theology. They co-authored *My Sister, My Brother*, a book on Black and womanist theologies in alternate chapters. Garth Baker-Fletcher also wrote *Xodus: An African-American Male Journey*, a book on Black theology, which I used in *The Nonviolent Atonement* as an example of second-generation Black theology. With their presentations in my seminar, they embodied black and womanist theology and the conversation between them. Garth told the seminar that my use of his book was the best response to his work by any author, Black or white. Karen Baker-Fletcher told the seminar that her class had thought my chapter on womanists had been written by a Black woman. It was reassuring to hear these affirmations of my understanding of Black and womanist theology.

JoAnne Marie Terrell, womanist professor from Chicago Theological Seminary, spoke in my theology class as well as in the weekly forum. The class met in the second- floor room of Centennial Hall with large, double, horseshoe-shaped seating. I did not tell Professor Terrell what I had previously said in class, but my suggestion for her class presentation was to provide a womanist critique of classic theological formulas. "They need to hear a womanist perspective," I said. "Give the class your womanist critique of Nicene Christology and Anselmian atonement."

As I had hoped, what Professor Terrell said echoed my own previous class lectures. From my position on a curve in the outside row, I could watch the class of some twenty students respond to Professor Terrell's comments. As the students realized what she was saying, a noticeable ripple went through the class, and knowing smiles appeared on their faces—they were proud of recognizing that they had heard it before. The next day, when I asked for their response to JoAnne Terrell, it was clear that hearing the critique of classic statements from a "real womanist" had raised significantly their appreciation of the course.

I also had a question for Professor Terrell. Knowing that Nicene and Chalcedonian Christology are raised to the category of transcendently true, unquestioned givens in the standard approach, I asked her if there was any theology that could not be revised. Her answer was direct and dramatic. "God never wrote any theology," she said. "All theology was written by people (and until very recently by men), and anything written by people can be revised." Since then, "God never wrote any theology" has become a part of my theological analysis and critique of the standard formulas.

A particular highlight was the visit of Cornel West, public philosopher and theologian from Princeton University. I picked Professor West up at the airport in Toledo. On the way to Bluffton, we chatted amiably, and he asked questions about my research and about Bluffton College. When I escorted West into a packed Founders Hall, the gymnasium with its tier of seats that held perhaps 1,200 people, the crowd applauded.

West looked up at the bank of people, turned to me, and said, "I'll be here as long as they want to ask questions." When West got up to speak, he displayed his ability to animate a crowd. He started by praising "The great leadership of President Lee Snyder, the first woman to be president of a Mennonite college." He came out from behind the podium, bowed to her, and led the audience in applause.

Then he moved on to "J. Denny Weaver," drawing out each syllable like a professional basketball announcer, "the greatest living Mennonite theologian, whom my friend of thirty-five years, Stanley Hauerwas, has not yet responded to," all said with great emotion, hands in two-handed point, and bowing to me. The audience exploded in thunderous applause.

Cornel West spoke for an hour about the juncture of racism and poverty and answered questions for another hour. After that he spent an hour at a reception in Marbeck Center, at which he signed books and talked with everyone in a crowded gallery. It was a memorable evening.

The visit of Cornel West came one year before I retired from Bluffton College. His visit in particular, and this series of guest speakers all together, constitute some of my best memories from this epoch in my career at Bluffton. These visitors made significant contributions to campus discussions as well as plugging into my theological agenda. With the extended conversations, I became more convinced than ever about the viability of my specific suggestion for nonviolent atonement, and using a narrative approach to writing theology that reflected the peace church but addressed all Christians.

Again in terms of the outline's chess metaphor, the affirmations I received would lead to significant new moves. But these conversations also make quite clear that developing theology is well beyond an individual activity. I was learning from engaging in a conversation that others were carrying on as well, and it involved significant mutual learning, with awareness of a wide audience.

In 2004, President Snyder initiated changing the name of Bluffton College to Bluffton University. A variety of developments both internal and external made the change appropriate. Under the leadership of President Snyder and Dean Kampen, Bluffton College had attained an unprecedented status in the history of the institution. Enrollment peaked at more than a thousand students; additions were made to the faculty; faculty were engaged in scholarship; Bluffton's profile improved as a Mennonite institution and as an academic institution.

Within the United States, the name *university* became an issue of distinguishing a four-year, liberal arts institution from technical schools who began calling themselves colleges. Additionally, abroad, the designation "university" was important to distinguish an institution of higher education from institutions in many countries where "college" designates a high school or even a grad school. Bluffton's name change was celebrated on 4 September 2004 with an exciting football game, a reception for the public with diverse food tables, and an impressive fireworks display.

When I retired in May 2006, I was proud to retire from Bluffton University, and grateful to Lee Snyder and John Kampen for a stimulating and productive final decade. Meanwhile, this decade was full of other meaningful life events as well.

20

Tilting at Windmills

Previous chapters referred to my book *The Nonviolent Atonement*. Its writing followed a number of years of learning about the function of violence and nonviolence in theology, along with collecting literature of black, feminist, and womanist theologians. In my theology classes, I rehearsed what I was learning from these sources, and how it contributed to my own development of a nonviolent atonement image. When a student asked what I wanted to accomplish with my view of atonement, I surprised myself by saying out loud that I wanted to be known as the man who overturned Anselm.

With the arrival of my sabbatical in the 1999-2000 academic year, I was prepared for a major presentation of my understanding. The plan was to write the book that would be the culmination of my learning about atonement, the book that would reject and then pose an alternative to the dominant, accepted-as-standard view of atonement inherited from Anselm of Canterbury. The sabbatical from Bluffton College would support one semester's release from teaching. I applied for a grant from the Louisville Institute that would cover the second half of the year. Both President Lee Snyder and Dean John Kampen played roles in the developmental stages of the book.

My initial application was turned down, but the refusal came with an invitation to resubmit after restructuring the outline. Dean John Kampen, who had much more experience with grants than I did, had given me good advice on the way to shape my proposal. Stress that your book will expand the intercultural awareness of Mennonites, he advised. Now with the refusal and invitation to resubmit in hand, I made an appointment to see the dean and walked across campus to his office in the administration building. I entered and without saying a word, I handed him the letter from the Louisville Institute. Dean Kampen read the letter. He looked up at me. After a couple seconds he said, "You are lucky. They want to fund it, and they told you how to restructure the outline." I smiled. "That is what I thought," I said. "I just wanted to verify with someone who knew more about grants than I do."I left his office very happy.

I have always enjoyed making revisions more than writing a first draft. The revision of the proposal to the Louisville Institute was the most fun I ever had working on a revision. I sent it off and in mid-morning on 9 June 1999, I received a phone call from John Lewis at the Louisville Institute. He informed me that the executive committee had approved my grant. Needless to say, I was elated. The funds from Louisville plus the half-year's sabbatical salary from Bluffton College meant that I had the entire 1999-2000 school year to devote to the project.

The college jumped at the opportunity for favorable publicity. I sat with the representative of the public relations department to help write a press release. For the grant application, I used a title that I hoped would attract the attention of the proposal evaluators. A provision of receiving the grant was that the Louisville Institute and the title of the grant would be named in any publicity materials. Thus the press release from Bluffton College mentioned "Christian Theology After Divine Child Abuse." The release went to the usual outlets, including the newspaper *Mennonite Weekly Review*, where it appeared in the 15 July 1999 issue. We soon learned that "divine child abuse" was like the proverbial red flag to a bull.

Following issues of *MWR* carried irate letters, denouncing the professor who believed in divine child abuse. The letters continued. Soon letters appeared that defended me, reminding readers that as yet I had not written the book, and that the angry folks should wait to see what the book actually said before condemning me. This barrage of letters to the editor took on a life of its own, appearing for the next four months.

I received visitors from off campus who wanted to verify that I was rejecting the traditional view, and I received personal letters that challenged me. One in particular came from J. Otis Yoder, a well-known, elderly fundamentalist whose group also published a monthly periodical. He took a brotherly tone, even while informing me that his board was planning to offer a critique, and advising me that it would not be favorable.

I wrote a letter to Yoder and explained that I had not yet written the book, but I listed several of my writings that he could consult in the meantime. Since I knew that presidents do not like surprises, before mailing the letter I showed it to my president, Lee Snyder. I supported her unreservedly, and I wanted to give her a heads-up on the coming rebuke and my response to it.

I secured an appointment to chat in President Snyder's office. A visitor saw a smiling, open face with rimless glasses, framed by brown hair cut short, seated behind a large desk. Aware of the negative publicity that I had attracted, I started by apologizing for causing the controversy and the bad publicity. She just laughed. "It's nothing like what I dealt with in my last position," she said. Then she asked if I could show her some of the positive memos I had received. "Of course," I said. "Good. I will quote them when I receive a complaint about you."

But the president was not finished. She continued, "The response to your work shows that its time is right. Few authors are fortunate to be able to write in that spot. I think it's wonderful." On a different occasion, President Snyder said that she saw letters of complaint she received "as challenges, as opportunities to teach people something."

Lee Snyder's final comment reminded my why she was a president and I was not. She told me not to send my letter to J. Otis Yoder as written. Giving him a list of titles, she said, "would merely ensure that he quoted them—and in the worst possible light." Instead, I should merely thank him for his brotherly warning, remind him that I had not yet written anything, and suggest that he "might want to wait to reply until he had read the finished book." The president's advice was correct on all counts. I sent the letter she suggested, and I never heard from J. Otis Yoder again.

My project struck a positive note with others. Letters in *MWR* welcomed a challenge to standard "blood atonement" and expressed eagerness to read my coming book. Alongside the letters in *MWR* that defended me, I received emails of support. For example, a Mennonite pastor in Tucson, Arizona wrote an encouraging memo and attached a sermon that demonstrated his agreement. A professor at Huntington College had received some of my articles from his dean of students, who was a Mennonite. This professor invited me to speak on atonement at Huntington. In July, when I walked around the national Mennonite Church-General Conference Mennonite Church convention in St. Louis, I received many positive comments from folks who had read about my project.

I had successfully persuaded the Louisville Institute that I had a viable project. I was now starting to write the book that I had long dreamed about, and I was scared. What if my finished project fell short of the expectations raised by having received a major grant and the recent publicity? What if once I started to write, the answer was less clear than I had projected in my proposal? And what if I could not find a good publisher?

I usually did my writing in my college office, but for this project I worked at home, away from colleagues who would chat, away from the temptation of the daily coffee sessions. I did not have a real study at home; my computer sat on a desk in a lesser-used sitting room. Each day, I brewed a fresh pot of coffee and selected a favorite from one of my 225-plus souvenir coffee mugs. I turned off all the lights on the first floor of the house except the one by the computer desk, left the daily newspaper unread, and focused on my computer screen and the task at hand. It was a tense and intense six months.

Since this manuscript entered new, potentially controversial territory, I sent it for evaluation to several contacts I had made in the academic network. I received affirmations and encouragement from Leanne Van Dyk at Western Theological Seminary, Walter Wink from Auburn Theological Seminary in New York, Delores Williams from Union Seminary in New York, and Ted Grimsrud at Eastern Mennonite University. I had called my new atonement image "historicized Christus Victor."

Leanne Van Dyk suggested that I use the term "narrative Christus Victor." I welcomed the suggestion and was pleased to implement it.

Among these readers, only Stanley Hauerwas from Duke University expressed a negative view of the manuscript. He wrote that what I did I did well, but that he had major disagreements. He said that I was too hard on Nicene orthodoxy and too close to liberal feminism. I made no changes in the manuscript on the basis of Hauerwas' comments. As a result of the affirmations, I became more convinced than ever of the viability of my argument.

At the annual meeting of the American Academy of Religion, I discussed the manuscript with a number of publishers. Three expressed serious interest. I had two offers and one still pending when I opted to go with the Wm. B. Eerdmans Publishing Co. It turned out to be an excellent decision.

The Nonviolent Atonement appeared in fall of 2001, with a full statement of my nonviolent atonement based on the Gospels, writings of Paul, and the book of Revelation, and then separate chapters on additional learning from black, feminist, and womanist theology.

Along with many thanks for the book, I received invitations to speak. Invariably after a presentation in which I described the abusive image of Anselmian atonement and divine child abuse, a woman in the audience would express thanks and say how good it was to hear a man discuss these issues. One such comment came from a Seventh Day Adventist woman, who attended an all-day, ecumenical colloquium sponsored by London Mennonite Center with sixty registrants from across the United Kingdom. She said she had counseled abused women, and "what you said about the harmful dimension of Anselmian atonement is very real. Don't allow anyone to tell you to stop saying it." Another was the comment by a woman at First Mennonite Church of Champaign-Urbana, Illinois, who after hearing that the church could abandon its abuse-provoking theology, told me "I have decided to give the church another chance."

After a session of the biennial convention of Mennonite Church USA, a senior-age pastor told me that the idea of God needing Jesus' death had never made sense to him, and he had long avoided preaching at Easter. "You explained why I was uncomfortable," he said, "and now I can preach again at Easter."

I was invited to spend two days with a class of twenty-four Doctor of Ministry students at now-closed Seabury-Western Theological Seminary in Chicago. The director of the program told me, "Impersonate your book," in other words, tell us what you wrote. I received many warm thanks from the class. One woman asked rhetorically, "Why haven't we heard this before?" I enjoyed a quite different response from a sixteen-year-old boy. In a sermon I had described Jesus' breaking of norms, in particular his healing the withered hand on the Sabbath. The boy's mother reported her son's comment, "Jesus was kind of a smart alec, wasn't he?" With the many affirmations of my critique of Anselmian or satisfaction atonement, I was grateful to Rebecca Parker and Rita Nakishima Brock, from whom I first learned the insight I conveyed.

In November 2002, at the annual meeting of American Academy of Religion in Toronto, Ontario, I was one of four presenters to speak on recent developments in atonement theology in a session sponsored by the Evangelical Theological Group of the AAR. My presentation was based on *The Nonviolent Atonement*. I faced a packed room. I learned later that 140 people had crowded into a room with chairs for 100, and additional folks who could not get in had been turned away. Sparked by the feminist challenge to Anselmian atonement and responses by defenders of the traditional view, atonement was clearly a hot topic among academicians.

Hans Boersma, a professor from Regent College in Vancouver, British Columbia, spoke ahead of me. He made a critical review of my book, defending an Anselmian, satisfaction approach, and arguing that I had missed a valuable tool by dismissing violence. When I got to the podium, I ad libbed, "Some folks really love violence." The audience laughed. I launched into my paper. It flowed. My ad libs clicked. I felt the audience with me, heads nodding at important points. Several times a line generated applause, a rare happening in such an academic setting. In the discussion period, questions were many and supportive. My answers resonated. The final question was an encouraging comment from Rebecca Parker, an author of the chapter in which I had first learned about divine child abuse. After the session, the stack of copies of my presentation disappeared quickly. I took email addresses from additional folks who wanted a copy of the paper. Many people came to shake hands and thank me for the presentation.

An individual who made a point of working through the crowd to speak to me was Rebecca Parker. Amid the jostling crowd, she gave me a heartwarming compliment: "You are one of the few men who actually uses feminist theology." By now she was a writing partner with Rita Nakashima Brock. After I heard the two of them make a joint presentation in a later session, they introduced me to their friends as "a colleague in the fight against atonement." I was still awed to be included as a participant in their struggle against the abusive dimensions of atonement theology.

In follow up to the AAR session, John Sanders, a theological professor from Hendrix College, edited expanded versions of the presentations into the book *Atonement and Violence*. For this publication, each speaker also wrote a response to the other speakers. Among other critiques leveled against my view, Boersma wrote that I had contradicted myself since my version of nonviolent activism actually assumed effective violence. He argued that such things as opposing a child's will in discipline or Jesus' breaking of the Sabbath by healing were actually instances of the employment of violence. My reply used the idea of the two continua that I had first articulated several years earlier in the conversation with J. Lawrence Burkholder. Thus, I wrote that Boersma saw everything on one continuum when in fact there were two continua, and one of those envisioned increasing pressure without resorting to harm or damage.

As the initial response to the grant makes clear, responses to *The Nonviolent Atonement* were not uniformly positive. Two reviews frame responses to the book. On the one hand, according to some folks, whatever success the book has comes at a high cost indeed. Conservative reviewer David McWilliams, writing about the book in the *Westminster Theological Journal*, used a

Bible citation to give his final evaluation of my rejection of the received satisfaction image of atonement: "Yet it was the will of the Lord to crush him; he has put him to grief" (Isa. 53:10). In other words, I had challenged what the reviewer considered the one and only, transcendently true means of salvation, and thus he pronounced me damned.

On the other hand, I relished the very supportive review by Catholic scholar Colby Dickinson writing in *Louvain Studies*. He suggested that if Anselmian atonement would no longer convince readers today, "We may have J. Denny Weaver's book to thank for that." The cheeky and audacious comment I once made in class, the seemingly impossible tilt at windmills, had taken on an air of reality.

21

Faith and Order Conversations

In July 2004, Ann Riggs phoned and invited me to give a presentation on Christology at a conference the following October for a meeting of the Faith and Order Commission of the National Council of Churches. The invitation triggered uncomfortable memories of earlier conversations but culminated in an exciting conference.

I first met Ann Riggs in June 2001, when we chatted about Quaker ecclesiology at a conference of Historic Peace Churches, held at the Bienenberg Bible School in Switzerland. This conference occurred in the context of the Decade to Overcome Violence declared by the World Council of Churches. At that conference I made a presentation on nonviolent atonement and the gospel of peace. Riggs was also an editor of *Seeking Cultures of Peace*, the book that published presentations from the conference.

The invitation to address the Faith and Order Commission was not my first awareness of it. In September 1983, John Howard Yoder sent me a carbon copy of a letter in which he suggested another Mennonite scholar or me as the Mennonite representatives to the Faith and Order Commission. Later I learned that Tom Finger, a fellow Mennonite theologian who follows a line much closer to standard orthodoxy than I do, was named as the representative.

Six years later, in October 1989 I attended a Faith and Order conference in Boston on the question of whether the Nicene

Creed could serve as a unifying formula for all churches. Tom Finger was a co-chair of the conference, and A. James Reimer, theology professor from Conrad Grebel College, well known for arguing that Mennonites should stand on standard Nicene orthodoxy, represented Mennonites on the program. The speakers, including Reimer, all strongly supported the Nicene Creed.

Because Reimer's paper mentioned me as a Mennonite who was wrong on Nicea, I was invited to the conference to give a five-minute response. My remarks mentioned the contextual character of the creed and the Constantinian shift, believers church ecclesiology, and asked whether there might be alternatives to Nicea's ontological categories for Christology. In that brief statement, I accomplished little more than demonstrating that I was an outlier.

Donald Dayton, holiness scholar and professor at then-Northern Baptist Theological Seminary, expressed his frustration to me that issues I raised were not picked up by the conference. The most egregious response to my remarks came from a well-known professor of ethics who called Emperor Constantine "a sign of God's providential guidance of the church," argued that nothing in the church changed with Constantine's conversion to Christianity, and implied that there were no other categories for Christology besides the ontological categories of Nicea.

Fifteen years after these conversations about the Nicene Creed at the meeting of the Faith and Order Commission, Ann Riggs' invitation indicated that the theological world had shifted. Now employed by the Commission, Riggs was organizing a conference to process the question "Do we need a new Christology?" and she asked me to present one of the three position papers. When she called, I had a number of other projects going, and squeezing in another major paper seemed difficult. I told her I would have to think about it for a couple days. Then Riggs told me the name of the theologian who she would ask if I said no. I did think—about the markedly different result this alternative would produce, and I thought about all the other folks that Riggs could have asked. I realized that she had placed me at the head of the list of Mennonite, peace-church theologians, and that this was an offer that I could not refuse. I would need to figure out how to make it work. I called Ann Riggs back and told her that I was glad to accept.

The consultation with the Faith and Order Commission met at Fuller Theological Seminary in October 2004. The program had three main speakers. I led, followed by Catholic scholar Arthur Kennedy, and womanist theologian Jacqueline Grant. In my presentation, I critiqued the Nicene tradition for the absence of ethics, which reflected its genesis in the Constantinian church. I explained my alternative approach, which developed Christology and nonviolent atonement from the narrative of Jesus, which produced a theology that was also intrinsically ethical.

George Hunsinger, theologian from Princeton Theological Seminary, gave the commissioned response. He said that he could affirm my attempt to link atonement, Christology, and ethics, but that was all. He called my effort sloppy, inappropriate, a poor analysis of historical theology, and added that arguing with tradition was not the way to engage in ecumenical discussion. By isolating my principle of nonviolence, Hunsinger continued, I had done violence to Nicea, whose context supplied its ethical dimension. He listed Tertullian, who died more than eighty years before the council of Nicea, as a source of the creed's ethics. He faulted me for not quoting Karl Barth and Martin Luther. Finally Hunsinger appealed to substitutionary atonement as a work of Christ that could not be repeated which, he said, undercut my statements about ethics and living out of the story of Jesus. Hunsinger concluded by saying that he did not have time to stay and converse because he had to leave to teach his class.

By this time in my career, I had long ceased being the uncertain theologian stunned by attacks such as those I had received from Ted VanderEnde or Ron Sider. By the time Hunsinger was done speaking, I had jotted down three quick points to make. As he walked across the back of the room, a bare fifteen feet from me, I called out to him to wait a moment, that I had three, sentence-long points to make. He ignored me, kept walking, and disappeared though the exit. I gave my three points to the audience: 1) I had established the narrative of Jesus as an ecumenical starting point accessible to all and Hunsinger had ignored it; 2) if the Nicene Creed contained the nonviolence of Jesus as Hunsinger had said, the church would long have been pacifist and we would not be having this conversation; 3) Hunsinger had not touched my point about the particularity or contextual nature of all theology.

Lunch break followed my paper and Hunsinger's response. Along with Fuller professors Glen Stassen and David Augsburger, whom I had previously known, many people told me that my presentation was clearly organized and insightful and Hunsinger's response troubling. Whether fairly or not, a woman I did not know used an impolite phrase to imply he was not of sound mind. Even years later, both Stassen and Augsburger recalled this event, called my presentation well done, and remained unsettled by Hunsinger's way of approaching the critique.

But there was more. Arthur Kennedy spoke immediately after the lunch break. His assigned topic was the emphasis on Peace in Vatican II. However, he took the first twenty minutes of his hour to ad lib a response to my presentation. Several times, he said, "Dennis had a point" about the particularity of theology, and summarized what I had said about developing alternatives. As he spoke, I kept waiting for a following "but on the other hand. . . ." But he did not have one. In other words, Catholic scholar Arthur Kennedy defended me without any explicit qualification.

This exchange reminded me of a small conversation between Catholics and Mennonites that I had participated in a few years previously. Similar to the Faith and Order conversation, the assigned topic was Christology, nonviolence, and the impact of the Constantinian church. I made an argument similar to the one to which Hunsinger objected. Mennonite scholars and theologians Walter Klaassen and Tom Finger objected strongly to my challenge to Nicene orthodoxy. In contrast I was defended by Monika Helwig, Catholic theologian at Georgetown University.

After the consultation at Fuller, the original plan was that Ann Riggs would publish the three presentations and the responses. Later I submitted a revised edition to a second editor who assumed work on the project. However, there were difficulties in obtaining the presentations from the other participants. Unfortunately, no published record was made of this conversation, and thus no formal account stands alongside *Faith to Creed* that published statements from the 1989 meeting. In any case, in this one instance at Fuller Theological Seminary, the positions of theological outlier and insider had been reversed!

22

Kenya and the Congo

Some years apart, I had opportunity to teach and lecture in two different educational settings. One was in Kenya and the other in the Congo. Neither experience unfolded as I had expected.

Kenya

In August 2001 I spent three weeks in Kenya, teaching a two-week term in a school for ministers sponsored by Regions Beyond Ministry (RBM). The opportunity arrived at the end of the sabbatical when I wrote *The Nonviolent Atonement*. RBM is a program run by Kenyans for Kenyans, with offices in Thika along with a retreat center at nearby Ngoliba. It was founded by leaders influenced by the charismatic and Protestant East African Revival.

Lynn Miller, a friend and fellow member of First Mennonite Church in Bluffton, had taught in the school. He reported that they needed some theological diversity, and urged me to volunteer. I thought that the school director had expressed a need for theological diversity, but it was actually Lynn acting on his own. In any case, I welcomed the chance to go to sub-Sahara Africa. I offered to volunteer at the school and received the invitation. I arrived in Thika with no idea what I was getting into.

I showed up a few days early for the two-week course. I spent two days with the director, and then two days with the prosperous pastor of a thriving mega church. In this pastor's house, the television set was tuned all day to Pat Robertson's TV network TBN. As I read on a comfortable sofa, I heard evangelistic calls and faith healing sessions. One day, I heard three different segments in which a host interviewed Hal Lindsey, who was billed as "a great student of prophecy." Lindsey said things like, "If Palestinians don't support Israel, it is because they do not read their Bibles." These days gave me a sense that the students I would encounter at the school for ministers likely had some familiarity with evangelicalism from the United States, and otherwise would be conservative theologically.

Students at the school for ministers came from across Kenya to attend the school of RBM. They spoke a number of native languages, which meant that English was the only common language. The school for ministry was called a college, and the academic preparation of the best students was close to my students in Bluffton.

It turned out that my preparation for class was not what they expected. There was one other American teacher, who was supplied to them by the mission board of Conservative Conference Mennonites. This teacher told me that the students liked to have a class handout that included an outline and the important points. They would then take notes on this handout and take it home and repeat the course for their congregations. Unfortunately, I had made no outlines to hand out. This was a minor problem. I ended up writing a great deal on the blackboard for the students to copy down.

I came prepared to teach two classes, one on the history and development of Christology and one on the book of Revelation. For the first class sessions, I introduced myself to the classes of twenty students, and I learned that they were eager to take a class with an American professor, who was the first teacher at this school with a PhD.

With my introduction past, I began the Christology class in good liberal fashion by telling them that I wanted to learn from them as well as teach them. Thus I would lay out ideas for them, and then we would discuss them. I went to the small blackboard and wrote "My Assumptions" and started to list them so that they would know the perspective from which I spoke. When I finished I asked for questions.

Hands shot up.

"If you do not know what you are teaching, why are you here?"

"If you do not teach firm truth, how can we convert Muslims? And Catholics?"

I talked about the different perspectives that we brought to a discussion and about the importance of understanding context. I explained that since Christianity and Islam each made ultimate claims, there was no further higher order of truth that would prove Christianity's superiority over Islam, and if there were it would actually be a higher truth than Christianity.

I made no headway with such explanations; I was having trouble "translating" what I intended to say. The cultural misunderstandings went both ways—I was misunderstanding how to teach them, and I was not what they expected in a teacher. With their help, I learned that for them, when I said "assumptions," they thought that I was laying out mere "guesses" and "maybes." In contrast, the students wanted answers in religion to be based on "firm faith." Finally after fifteen or twenty minutes, I realized that the situation called for drastic action. I erased the blackboard and told the class "Forget everything I just said." I announced that I was going to start the class over.

I went to the blackboard and wrote, "My firm convictions" and I listed such comments as "I believe the Bible is the source of truth" and "Jesus is the source of salvation." With this approach, I could start the class, but still one student had a question. "If those are your firm convictions, why didn't you give those to start with?" I pleaded "Cultural differences." Later I learned that the students talked to the director about me and this class session. He told them that in the United States they did things differently than in Kenya.

Once I had quieted the firestorm about assumptions versus firm convictions, the course went along well. I talked about the history of the development of Christology from the New Testament to the Council of Chalcedon. The students seemed interested. They did want to learn.

One surprise came when I mentioned the stories in which Jesus confronted injustice and indicated that such stories still served today as examples to confront injustice. I quickly learned that the idea that Jesus confronted injustice and served as a model for today was new material for them. What they knew about Jesus was that God sent him to die for their sins. I received two responses. The majority gave me some version of "Jesus came to die for sins," and what I said sounded like "heresy." One man had a different perspective. "Today," he said, "you may have started a revolution."

These two responses reflect another conversation. When I raised a question about traditional theology that supported colonial occupation, the response was that colonialism may have been bad, "but at least it brought us the gospel." In retrospect, this comment stands out in contrast to what I heard in the Congo, as the next section of this chapter relates.

A further surprise came at the beginning of the final class period, when I introduced them to Black theology. I had assumed that they would be thrilled to learn of theology written by Black scholars, a theology that critiqued colonialism and racism. Wrong assumption. I had no sooner commenced to talk about Black theology than the vociferous response came: "This is heresy. Why are you giving us this heresy?" I dropped the subject of Black theology and ad libbed something for the rest of the period.

My class in the book of Revelation had other kinds of surprises. In general, for many people the book of Revelation is a mysterious book full of fantastic images. A common assumption is that Revelation predicts the future. Long ago, I learned a "common sense" approach to Revelation, namely that it is beyond one's wildest imagination that a writer in the first century could be predicting events two thousand years in the future. If Revelation was to make sense to its first readers, common sense indicates that images in Revelation refer to events happening in the time of the writer, and that is where modern readers must begin to understand the book. With that approach, the images do refer to empire and emperors in the first century, and Revelation makes sense.

I went to the school for ministers at RBM with the assumption that they would know nothing about the book of Revelation and would thus be excited to learn how much sense Revelation can make when read from a common-sense perspective. Again, wrong assumptions on both accounts.

As I suspected after hearing TBN in the pastor's home the previous week, these students knew the text of Revelation as well or even better than I did. They were fully immersed in and believed the predictive approach; they were quick to ask me about the prediction implied in a particular verse.

When I began explaining how I would teach Revelation to the class, the students protested at once. The view I represented was heresy, they said. One student told me that what I said bothered him so much that he was considering withdrawal from the course. I plunged ahead, but my discussion of presuppositions, contexts, and frames of reference accomplished nothing. With five class days and ten hours of class remaining, I struggled to know how to make it through to the end.

In their minimal library, I found the four-volume *Interpreters Dictionary of the Bible*. The article on Revelation listed four approaches. I realized I could show them the four and explain that they were using the dispensational futurist approach whereas I was following a preterist or historicist approach. Because it was in a book, I could show them that my view had credibility—I was not just making it up. I told them that they did not have to believe me, but that for educational purposes they should know about my approach.

That got me to the end of the class. In the break, I overheard students discussing among themselves. Some said that they did not need to learn about this erroneous version, whereas others said that even if they did not believe it, they needed to know about it for their own educational purposes. The class did stay with me to the end of the term.

The term at the school of ministers ended on positive notes. The students all thanked me warmly for teaching them. They seemed enamored by the chance of learning from a "real" American professor. I was grateful for their words, despite our differences.

Some years later, I read Philip Jenkins' book, *The Next Christendom*, in which he described the rise of Christianity in the global south. I also heard him speak in a session at the American Academy of Religion. Jenkins said that North American liberals say that they want to listen to their brothers and sisters in the global south. But when they do, he said, they will not like what they hear, because this rising Christianity is fundamentalist, patriarchal, and anti-gay rights. In Kenya, I experienced a small sample of what Jenkins described.

The Congo

In 2009, Mary and I spent a month in the Congo (Kinshasa), hosted by Mennonite Central Committee. Suzanne Lind, a co-director of MCC in the Congo, arranged for me to present lectures in three university settings in Kinshasa—Université Chrétienne de Kinshasa (UCKIN); Université Protestante du Congo (UPC); Center Universitaire de Missiologie (CUM)—and the Institut Biblique in Kikwit, as well as to speak to a group of women theologians, to pastors in Kikwit, and to preach in one church service. My specific lecture subject was the atonement theology that appeared in my book *The Nonviolent Atonement*. This theology of atonement was definitely not that of United States fundamentalism and evangelicalism, but I was speaking with the support of the Mennonite Central Committee hosts. In light of my experience in Kenya eight years previously, I approached the lectures warily.

A Congolese associate of MCC translated my lectures into French. I read the lectures in French. Using the French that I had learned three decades earlier in Belgium and Algeria, I handled all the question-and-answer sessions in French.

At UCKIN, I spoke to sixty students in a room with a wide arc of tiered seats. At UPC, I lectured in a large cathedral-like chapel with 175 in the audience. At CUM, I learned that I was the guest speaker for Missions Week. I spoke from a stage to seventy students arrayed in desks below. Finally, in Kikwit at the Institut Biblique, I spoke to an audience of 100 in an open church, with the excited voices of children playing outside and chickens wandering in through the open doors.

When I began my first lecture, I had no idea what to expect. I forged ahead, launching into my critique of the standard images of atonement. Then I sketched the first segment of my alternative, which was to show how the narrative of Jesus was an atonement image of confronting evil, which killed him, but God raised him in a victory for the reign of God. When I asked for questions, many hands shot up across the array of sixty students in the small auditorium.

The first student I called on posed an excellent question. He understood exactly what I had said, and asked about my understanding of violence, and the story of Jesus cleansing the temple, which has been used to justify violence. I was unsure how I would do ad libbing answers in French, but there was nothing to do but start talking and see what happened. It seemed a bit complicated, but I explained the two continua of violence and nonviolence that I had first articulated in response to J. Lawrence Burkholder.

Fortunately the word *continuum* exists in both English and French. I explained that the temple cleansing belonged on the continuum of nonviolence. I made it through the rather complicated answer. The questioner smiled and nodded appreciatively. I took more questions. And as I realized that I could deal with questions in French, I relaxed and enjoyed the occasion.

My experience in the several venues in the Congo produced a kaleidoscope of memories, observations, and learnings, some unique, some repeated between institutions. In the lectures in all four settings, I emphasized that Jesus is an example of nonviolent advocacy. I said that his death was not needed by God, but was the result of evil that opposed the will of God. Thus our calling as Christians is to join with Jesus in confronting the evil in the world, and witnessing to the reign of God. This message about following Jesus in confronting evil was the one that students in Kenya heard with suspicion, but no one in the Congo challenged me on that message. On the contrary, the students in the Congo welcomed this message warmly. I was overwhelmed by the response.

In my critique of traditional atonement imagery, I emphasized that the passive Jesus who submitted to unjust suffering of satisfaction atonement was not a good model for a woman abused by her husband. Then when I explained that slaves had been told to be like Jesus and submit to masters, and that in countries like the Congo people were encouraged to submit to the injustice of colonialism, audiences resonated and welcomed the image of the activist Jesus who confronted injustice.

I learned that the Congolese are largely an oral culture. Students do not take a lot of notes. My MCC hosts told me to watch how the students sat during a lecture. As I looked around an audience, I saw many students sitting with arms crossed, looking directly at me. In the United States, arms crossed might be a show of displeasure, a sign of shutting the speaker out. In Congo, it meant, "I am fully devoted to what you are saying."

The students paid attention and asked insightful questions, as good or better than any seminary classes I have addressed in the United States. I was impressed with the Congolese ability to listen to lectures and comprehend and draw implications. After every lecture, the host of the session summarized what they had heard. These summaries were excellent, as good as any summary I could have written about the lecture. Repeatedly the summaries said that I had given them permission to think outside of or beyond traditional theology, and therefore they now had permission to begin thinking about theology in their own context. In Kikwit, the leader's summary told the audience that they had been exposed to a "Mennonite Jesus by a real Mennonite professor," and that as Mennonites they should follow this activist Jesus.

The students genuinely appreciated the lectures and the academic tone that they took. After one set of lectures, I overheard a student say, "He gave us real theology, not like the missionaries." I overheard another student say, "C'est la théologie moderne, il faut s'adapter." (This is modern theology, we need to adjust to it.) After a lecture, a student noted that I had challenged traditional theology, which led him to ask, "Êtes vous révolutionnarire ou conservateur comme les missionnaires?" (Are you revolutionary or conservative like the missionaries?) I told him that I was *révolutionnaire*, an answer that pleased him.

In each setting, I talked about the changes in the church symbolized by Constantine, including the fact that the church had come to accommodate the sword, and reviewed the theological changes that followed, including creedal statements that avoided ethics, and the emergence of satisfaction atonement that modeled passive submission to injustice. At CUM, the dean who hosted my lectures has a PhD from Trinity International in Chicago. His response could have been made by most conservative Evangelicals in the United States—a recitation of standard talking points of Nicene and Chalcedonian Christology and Anselmian atonement but without responding to my critiques of these doctrines. After the sessions, students lined up to shake hands and thank me for coming. One young woman fully made my day. She stopped the line to have her picture taken with me. Then she said, "Je suis tout à fait d'accord avec vous." (I am in complete agreement with you.) "What you said makes more sense than anything I have heard from professors here."

I made a significant observation about the impact of social context during this trip. When I spoke in contexts with few resources, the questions about the implications of Jesus' confrontation of evil, and victory in the resurrection, concerned poverty and suffering. In situations with more resources, the questions about implications tended to deal with politics and the political situation in the Congo.

These questions about the implications of an activist Jesus for poverty or politics had an additional dimension. In the setting of the large cathedral-like building with 175 students at UPC, in the question-and-answer period a student asked what Jesus' confrontation of injustice implied for their political setting in Kinshasa. I was embarrassed. I had not done enough reading to have any sense of politics. I had no idea what to say. In my mind I gave what I considered a cop-out answer. I said, "Je ne veux pas et je ne peux pas vous dire comment l'appliquer. Vous devrez en décider vous-même." (I don't want to and I can't tell you how to apply it. You will have to decide that for yourselves.)

The host of the meeting was chair of the theology department, an erudite Congolese scholar who had spent seven years teaching theology in Germany. After that answer, he leaned into his microphone and said a resounding "Amen." Then in his summary, he said, "Listen to what this American professor has said; he said that you *can* figure out how to confront the problems here." To my relief, my answer given in ignorance turned out to be a good answer.

In a setting with fewer resources, I had a parallel exchange. In Kikwit, in my answers to questions about activist Jesus and poverty, I stressed God's presence with them, and repeated the points about following an activist Jesus to confront unjust situations. A Mennonite conference leader talked to me after my last presentation for the Institut Biblique. As we stood in the shade of the building on the hot afternoon, he told me, "You do not know it, but you have been a tremendous blessing from God for us." He explained that the missionaries taught "blessed are the poor." The missionaries did everything—teaching, giving clothes, supplying money for churches, and more. Our people are poor, he said, and they are still sitting around, waiting for God's blessing. We are trying to teach them that they need to work to help God's blessing. He concluded, "Your statement that we need to work with Jesus to confront injustice is exactly what we needed." Again, my comment had been helpful apart from my intent.

Both the comment about figuring out for themselves how to confront political injustice, and the statement about needing to work to help God's blessing, reflect the different dimensions of the colonial legacy of "learned helplessness." The Congo suffered greatly under the colonial regime of Belgium, an oppression whose impact continues to the present. (For that story, read *King Leopold's Ghost* by Adam Hochschild.) One dimension of colonial domination over the Congo was convincing the Congolese that only white people could make things happen. That idea still lingers, as when the dean told the students to listen to this American professor who said that they could confront the problems of Congo and the church leader in Kikwit who said that his people need to work to help God's blessing. It was an overwhelming experience to hear that in my ignorance I had actually done some good.

Conclusion

In Kenya, they liked me personally but received my message with reservations. It was an interesting, satisfying, and difficult two weeks. In the Congo, they liked me personally and accepted fully what I said. I left the Congo feeling like it was one of the peak experiences of my career. In both Kenya and Congo, these students heard material that was new or unexpected, different from their previous experience with visitors from North America. I can only hope that the classes and lectures planted a proverbial seed.

I cannot generalize very far from these two, small samples. However, one observation is that the French colonial language prevented the impact of American fundamentalist TV on the folks I met in the Congo.

23

Another Lesson

I retired from Bluffton University after the spring semester of 2006, and we moved to Madison, Wisconsin. Retirement provided opportunity to work on a number of projects. In October 2010 I began one of the more consequential of these projects, a book on John Howard Yoder, the professor whose book *Preface to Theology* had set my career-long theological direction when I first started to teach in 1974.

The decision was precipitated by the recent appearance of articles and a book that aggravated my longstanding concerns about interpreters such as Mark Thiessen Nation, then a theology professor at Eastern Mennonite Seminary, and Craig Carter, theology professor at Tyndale University in Toronto, who insisted—incorrectly, I believed—that Yoder's theology depended on so-called orthodox christological and trinitarian doctrine. My book would correct these interpretations. The book accomplished its intended purpose. In the process, I also learned a valuable lesson. It will not surprise that this chapter of the memoir was the most difficult one for me to write.

I first discussed the possibility of a book with my friend Earl Zimmerman, a colleague from the Mennonite academic network, who was spending a year in Madison as interim pastor of Madison Mennonite Church. Earl and I met frequently for lunch, often in True Café in Fitchburg, where I would get the special of half-sandwich and soup, or Jamerica on Willy Street, where I relished the mango-run-down catfish. In one of our luncheons, Earl and I developed a plan that included the focus of individual chapters and names of scholars who might contribute to the book. I tested the plan with other colleagues a few days later.

I wrote the first chapter, which traced Yoder's methodology in *Preface to Theology* to the published version of his keynote address from the 1980 conference on Christology at Bluffton College. My chapter displayed his relativizing of the classic terminology, showing that it was a human construct that reflected a particular context rather than being universally true, transcendent, unquestioned givens. In other contexts, Yoder implied, we could learn from, but need not be beholden to, these supposedly standard formulas in talking about Jesus.

In addition to this chapter, I co-wrote two other chapters that extended Yoder's theology into areas that he did not address. One with Gerald J. Mast showed how to take Yoder's methodology into other contexts and dealt with Black theology and post evangelical theology. Earl Zimmerman co-authored the second, which extended Yoder's discussion of the Jewish-Christian schism into conversation with Islam and Hinduism. I commissioned additional chapters on specific aspects of Yoder's thought.

Earl wrote his PhD dissertation on the sources of Yoder's theology and then published a revised version in the book series that I edited. One of Earl's chapters in our book used material from the dissertation, including a memo in which Yoder had discussed his methodology in a way that confirmed my analysis. Further, Earl used letters Yoder wrote during his doctoral work in Switzerland. These letters revealed that Yoder used a dissertation in Anabaptist history to develop an approach to theology that bypassed the standard theology. Thus Earl's chapter used historical analysis to display a conclusion that agreed with what I showed through analysis of Yoder's theological work.

For years, *Preface* existed in informal format, as lectures transcribed and distributed by Anabaptist Mennonite Biblical Seminary. It was posthumously edited into a formally published book. Many scholars bypassed it, thinking that was mere classroom lectures, while those like me who had actually heard the lectures as students at AMBS knew that it was the real key to Yoder's outlook. Our book made this clear.

Thirteen years older than I am, Yoder's reputation as a towering intellect had already established him as an iconic figure when I arrived in seminary in the mid-1960s. His physical appearance reflected that image. He stood perhaps 6 feet 5 inches, with dark hair, a gray goatee, and a steady gaze through horn-rimmed glasses when he lectured. He sometimes wore a deep tan sport coat, over a green vest sweater, brown tie on a dark shirt, with dark pants.

His resonant baritone, classroom voice and organized lectures belied his awkward social behavior. Stories abounded of both intellect and awkwardness. He read a book while walking along the street to his office. In an apocryphal story, he once tripped and fell, and lay on his back finishing the page before getting up. My father-in-law, also a seminary professor, described teaching Yoder Hebrew in the space of a Christmas break. He did not make small talk and might walk away from someone who tried.

As a highly organized person, Yoder served as president of the Goshen Biblical Seminary half of AMBS from 1970-73, but the story is told of a time the seminary hosted a group of visiting ministers. Colleagues suggested that Yoder bring greetings to the ministers. He entered the room; the ministers came to attention. He walked to the podium, said "Greetings," and walked out. Already fluent in French and German, the story was told of his acquiring Spanish when he taught a course in South America—he read a grammar book on the plane, worked with a translator the first week, was correcting the translator the second week, and lectured himself the remainder of the course.

Yoder's book *The Politics of Jesus* made *Christianity Today*'s list of the top ten books of the twentieth century. Overall he wrote seventeen books in five languages and published hundreds of articles. He was an influential, internationally known advocate of a pacifist worldview. He died December 30, 1997, the day after his seventieth birthday. The *New York Times* published his obituary.

Through the years I had brief, in-person interactions with Yoder at conferences, and he knew that I followed his theological lead. In 1996, he wrote to me with a critique of an article I had written for *The Gospel Herald*. In a short first paragraph, he acknowledged that I was attempting to follow in his line of thought. Then in more than an entire, single-spaced page, he explained what I had missed. Once I got over the shock of being corrected and digested his analysis, it enabled a major advance in my understanding of the particularity of theology.

Another time I asked Yoder if he thought that the symbolism in the book of Revelation portrayed images of the atonement image Christus Victor. To me, it was an original idea. Yoder replied that he had made that observation but never considered writing about it. If I thought it important, he said, I should go ahead. I did. It became an important element of my discussion of nonviolent atonement.

Suffice it to say that I held Yoder in high esteem. But cracks in the pedestal appeared publicly in 1991, when eight women accused Yoder of sexual abuse. A church commission determined that the charges were valid. Yoder was forbidden from speaking or publishing in church contexts. He submitted to a four-year disciplinary process (1992-1996), following which the commission pronounced themselves satisfied with the results, and he was restored to full service in the church.

It was a relief to have Yoder available again. We were organizing a conference at Bluffton College on postmodernity, and we were pleased to engage Yoder as keynote speaker. He accepted but died before the conference took place.

I heard rumors that some women were not satisfied with the way the abuse accusations had been handled by church authorities and that some thought that his writing should no longer be used. However, names of the eight accusers were not generally known, and none of the folks in my immediate circle made these arguments. At the time the problem thus seemed somewhat limited.

Yoder's methodology of developing theology out of the narrative of Jesus continued to influence my work, even as by the time of his death I was developing it in ways different from and apart from and beyond anything that he had done. I articulated a specific atonement image whereas Yoder refused to make final statements of theology. When I developed my understanding for a nonviolent God, I rejected Yoder's argument that the accounts in the Old Testament of divine commands to massacre enemies were about obedience rather than about killing.

Perhaps most important was my specific learning from groups on the margin of standard theology. Yoder went to South America to engage in dialogue with liberation theologians but never engaged with Black liberation theology or with womanist theologies in the United States. These theologies became important partners in my development of an atonement image. My embrace of feminist theology and the image of "divine child abuse" clearly did not come from Yoder.

I submitted our manuscript on John Howard Yoder to Herald Press in April 2012. Herald Press reviewers raised some questions. At least one reviewer believed that Yoder's theology depended on orthodox christological and trinitarian doctrine, the view that the book disputed. However, when I had handled all the comments, the book editor agreed that I had indeed satisfactorily dealt with the reviewers' questions, and the manuscript could now be published.

Nevertheless, after further considerations she informed me that it was too academic for their audience and would likely not sell the 2000 copies the first year that they needed for the book to break even. I contacted my editor at Wipf and Stock, who knew me as "the atonement guy." He snapped up the book immediately for the Cascade list, their highest academic imprint. It appeared in 2014.

Meanwhile, the delay during which I answered the critiques of Herald Press reviewers proved providential. In the interim while I worked on the revisions, it became apparent that many more than eight women had been accosted by Yoder. Many women were dissatisfied with and angry about how the disciplinary process had been handled by the church commission and by what appeared to be an ongoing disregard of women's perspective.

I was not aware of these developments when I asked Lisa Schirch, a professor of peace studies and conflict resolution at Eastern Mennonite University, to write a supportive blurb for the back cover of the book. In no uncertain terms she made clear the major problem with the book. We had ignored the abuse, she said, and we did not even include any women as writers. As constituted, the book was simply one more example of men preserving an icon and ignoring women's perspectives and women's issues. Far from the support I had expected, her words hit me like a hard punch to the gut.

However, having been sensitized by my previous work with feminist theology, I recognized the truth of Lisa Schirch's critique. I explained to Schirch that the book argued a specific case and there were no women who had written about that dimension of Yoder's thought. Ted Grimsrud and Gerald Mast wrote additional chapters on aspects of Yoder's abuse. After some contentious consultation with my colleagues, I asked Lisa to write an Afterword, which she graciously agreed to do. It serves as the book's final chapter.

The Afterword acknowledged the good work we had done with the book. Lisa noted that the chapter that Earl and I wrote on Yoder's treatment of the Jewish-Christian schism justified her marriage to a man of Jewish faith. But she cautioned that never again should anyone be attributed the iconic status that would render him impervious to challenges, and she made very clear the importance of listening to women's voices.

The book stands today as among the more authoritative books on the theology of John Howard Yoder. It is not a random collection of essays. The book makes an integrated argument about the radical, deep structure of Yoder's theology that begins with the six narrative identifiers of Jesus in the book of Acts, while also unfolding influences on him as disparate as sixteenth-century Anabaptism, Oscar Cullmann, and Karl Barth, and including chapters that extended Yoder's thought in directions he did not take. It concludes with Lisa Schirch's important warning about avoiding idolization and listening to the voices of victims.

It was necessary to consider the learning from Yoder that shaped my theological agenda in light of the scope of Yoder's abusive conduct. My primary learning and orientation came from the *Preface* lectures, which relativized the classic creedal statements and identified the sermons in Acts as a narrative foundation for Christology. This was an orientation and methodology that I could develop into a narrative approach to atonement and then expand beyond Yoder to incorporate black, feminist, and womanist theologies. I cannot simply unlearn what I have developed over the decades, and I continue to think in these terms in my theologizing.

At the same time, no methodology is exempt from misuse, and I am painfully aware that with that same starting point, Yoder attempted to justify his abusive behavior in some unpublished essays. My introduction to Yoder's thought through *Preface* was relatively rare. Many readers learned to know Yoder through his *Politics of Jesus*, and for them he became the preeminent pacifist ethicist. For these readers, I can understand that learning of the abusive conduct calls into question his peace theology, sometimes accompanied by calls to cease reference to Yoder's work.

We cannot simply unlearn or eliminate Yoder's influence any more than we can simply use his material and ignore the abuse. It seems, I suggest, that there is no either-or solution. It is certainly not required that theologians use or reference Yoder, but for those who do reflect his theological influence, the abuse must be included alongside use of the material.

No methodology is immune to abuse by an individual working alone. One safeguard against perversion of methodology, such as Yoder's manipulation of the biblical narrative to justify his abusive behavior, is to acknowledge one way that theology differs from the chess game that outlines this memoir. Different from chess, the practice of theology should always be done in public, with frequent checking of views with colleagues and even with those who disagree

Producing the book on the theology of John Howard Yoder turned into a painful experience. It also taught me an important lesson—namely how consequential it is to listen to the voices of victims, this time the many victims of the man whose thought started me on my career as a theologian and shaped my initial approach to theology more than four decades ago. It is a profound and conflicted and sorrowful legacy.

24

Still More

When I retired from Bluffton University, I looked at my many-faceted rejection of Anselmian, satisfaction atonement, and the development of a nonviolent atonement image as my primary theological contribution. It was particularly satisfying to have made this contribution in conversation with black, feminist, and womanist theologies. It may be that in the long view, if I am remembered at all, it will be for my writing on this atonement theology.

Meanwhile, a revised version of *Becoming Anabaptist* had just appeared, with expanded material on Hutterites and Anabaptists in Moravia, a new statement of meaning for the contemporary world, and an appendix that responded to the definition of Anabaptism in terms of a "core" common to all Anabaptists. In addition, the book with Gerald Mast that became *Defenseless Christianity* was in process as an effort to produce a new paradigm of Anabaptism. With these thoughts and products in mind, it seemed that retirement projects would consist mostly of the expansions of previous learning. However, the productive years that followed produced surprises as well as the instances of painful learning described in the previous chapter.

Retirement seemed to rush at us. Our plan had been to move in August 2006. However, the offer we could not refuse on our house required us to vacate the house by the Friday following the Sunday of Commencement on 7 May. This change of plan meant that the spring semester was harried. Throughout that last spring in Bluffton, Mary had worked on downsizing and packing up our house, while I worked at packing my office between meeting my classes, organizing guest speakers for the coming year, and grading term papers.

The Monday after commencement we finished packing both our house and my office. Tuesday, the moving truck came, and all our possessions were loaded for the journey to Madison, Wisconsin. The next day, Wednesday, we worked all day, cleaning the house we were leaving after thirty-one years. Thursday morning, 11 May 2006, we drove to our new home, a condo in Madison. Even in Madison, the rushed feeling continued. Since we had advanced our moving date by a couple months, the finishing work on our condo was still several weeks from completion.

Thus my first piece of writing in retirement was done sitting on a straight chair with my computer on a card table, and surrounded by seventy boxes of books, with the builder working in the next room to install book shelves in my future study. This first written product was an article commissioned for the German periodical, *Mennonitische Geschichtsblätter*. The assignment was to describe my approach to theology in the context of debates among North American Mennonite theologians. It appeared in the print edition of 2006.

The second item, still done on the card table and surrounded by boxes of books, was a presentation for the conference at AMBS on 9 and 10 June 2006 in honor of the tenth anniversary of the *Confession of Faith in a Mennonite Perspective*. After several revisions and efforts at publication that did not materialize, a revised and expanded version of this essay was finally published in the issue of *Anabaptist Witness* for May 2020. A mention in chapter 10 described its significance.

In May 2007 Mary and I assisted with a tour that took Bluffton University soccer players to Europe for exposure to soccer and church history. I served as historical resource person and Mary was the confidante of the women. We saw a European Cup match, toured a soccer stadium with moveable turf and watched a practice of AFC Ajax, the top team in Amsterdam. We visited the Menno Simons monument in Witmarsum. In Pingjum, we saw the hidden church and the first church that

Menno served as pastor, followed by a visit to the estate where he spent his final days. Along with Anabaptist sights in Amsterdam, we gazed at St. Lambert's church in Münster, on which cages with the disgraced Anabaptists had hung. We visited the Wartburg castle, where Martin Luther had spent ten months in hiding, during which he translated the New Testament into German. We spent a delightful half day in Wittenberg, visiting the Schloßkirche where Martin Luther is said to have posted the 95 *Theses* and where he is buried. We also toured the city church from which Karlstadt removed the icons, and ate lunch on the city square. I welcomed this review of Reformation history.

Our visit to Leipzig with the students reinforced one of my long-held beliefs. We visited the Nikolikirche (St. Nicholas Church), and the Stazimuseum, which once housed the headquarters of the East German secret police for the region. From participants in the events, we learned about the Revolution of the Candles. This movement began as prayer meetings for peace in the Nikolikirche and grew into the nonviolent movement that spread all over East Germany (officially the German Democratic Republic) and led to the collapse of the regime, the fall of the Berlin Wall in 1989, and the reunification of Germany.

When the regime fell, Stazi officials began destroying records. The revolutionary crowd occupied the building to stop that destruction; they still occupy it. The director of the Stasimuseum is a woman who entered with that original occupation. In essence, she had never left. This story of the prayer meeting that spread into a revolution stands for me as an important example of the role of the church in witnessing to nonviolent struggle, and the fact that nonviolence is a viable means of confronting injustice when people have the will to employ it, and a demonstration that freedom need not depend on violence.

My son-in-law Alain Epp Weaver and my friend Gerald Mast collaborated to produce a marvelous surprise for me. In July 2007, my wife Mary and I, two of our daughters and their families, and Gerald and his children shared the Sycamore Lodge during family camp at Camp Friedenswald in southern Michigan. The first evening, we were all together relaxing with snacks in the living room of the lodge. Alain got everyone's attention, and Gerald handed me a folder and said, "Denny, did you hear about this new book?" I opened the folder and discovered the title page, dedication page, and table of contents for a Festschrift that Alain and Gerald were editing in my honor. They had kept the secret as long as possible. Publisher Michael King's desire to start advertising required the announcement. The first copies would be available in the coming March, and there would be a launch for the Festschrift at Homecoming at Bluffton University in May 2008. I had expected that something like this might happen, but this production was well beyond anything I had imagined—twenty chapters and an academic publisher, along with a public ceremony.

An important element of collaboration with Gerald Mast that came to fruition soon after our move to Madison was editing his revised dissertation as a volume in the C. Henry Smith Series. Editing this manuscript continued our mutual learning unabated. The book appeared in 2006 as *Separation and the Sword in Anabaptist Persuasion.*

The year 2009 brought two opportunities abroad that made significant contributions to my theological convictions. In March we were in the Congo. That story appears in an earlier chapter. Then in October I spent a month in Germany at the invitation of Fernando Enns, Mennonite theology professor in Hamburg and Amsterdam. On this trip, I avoided speaking English as much as possible, and worked on using the German that I had learned forty years earlier. My lectures were translated into German, I read them in German, and attempted to respond to questions in German.

By the time I left Germany, I was handling all question-and-answer sessions in German. During this time, I was guest speaker at the annual study conference of the South German Mennonite conference, gave lectures and presentations in Regensburg, Frankfurt, Heidelberg, and Bammental, spoke with faculty at the Bienenberg in Basil, and preached in three different churches. In these venues, I encountered great interest, insightful questions, and received many affirmations. I returned home once again with the sense that the theology I had developed made an important contribution to the contemporary church.

On this trip I was also updated on another project initiated by Fernando Enns, namely a translation of *The Nonviolent Atonement* into German. It appeared in 2016 as *Gewaltfreie Erlösung*.

I served as Faculty Athletic Representative (FAR) at Bluffton University for twenty-two years. In the official elements of the role, I represented our institution at the quarterly meetings of our athletic conference and at the annual meeting of the National Collegiate Athletic Association (NCAA). Unofficially, my role was to translate between athletic staff and coaches, and the academic faculty, who at times misunderstood each other.

Once in a while, someone would question how I could support competitive athletics and play handball myself while also advocating nonviolence. I gave the answer I sketched earlier in this memoir. When athletes compete within the rules and with respect for their opponents, each side is stimulating the other to play better and to improve their skills. When done right, rather than being an implicitly aggressive or even violent activity, competitive athletics is a cooperative activity, and I was glad to support the Athletic Department.

On 9 August 2010, I received a phone call from Phill Talavinia, the Athletic Director at Bluffton University. The call itself was not unusual. In my roles as FAR, I traveled to the meetings with Phill, and also consulted with him on campus issues. Even after my move to Madison, he sometimes called to get my opinion on an issue. Thus I was not surprised when Phill began the call by describing the process they had gone through to upgrade the school mascot, the beaver. They had retired the old beaver costume for a year, and then hired a firm to design a new costume and image that could be introduced with some fanfare. The firm they engaged designed mascots for major league baseball and NFL football teams, major universities, and more. Along with a new costume, the firm also asked what they wanted to symbolize with the name of the beaver. Phill explained that the university wanted a name that would link together the athletic and academic sides of the school.

Up to that point, I thought that Phill was going to ask my advice on the name or perhaps give a couple names and ask my preference. But that is not what he said. He continued, "You represent both the academic and athletic sides. We want to name the mascot J. Denny Beaver." Was I okay with that, he asked. For a moment I could not speak. I was simply overcome, dumbfounded at being honored in this way. I stammered out, "Okay, if that is what you want. Do it."

In early October that year, I attended homecoming weekend at Bluffton University to meet J. Denny Beaver. The public relations people arranged a scenario in a food tent, with J. Denny Beaver going through the crowd with my picture, asking if anyone had seen me. We met, and pictures were snapped. I autographed a copy of *The Nonviolent Atonement* for J. Denny. I enjoyed the event greatly.

The fun continues. On occasion, international contacts mention J. Denny Beaver. People who have no knowledge of theology are pleased to know about J. Denny Beaver. Or, at a church conference, a parent will bring a shy child who wants to meet the man for whom the beaver is named. I enjoy the humorous notoriety of the likely unique status of being the only person for whom a mascot is named.

In February 2011, major events in Madison intersected with my theological understanding of nonviolent activism. Republican Governor Scott Walker, with support of the Republican-controlled legislature, proposed a budget that eliminated the rights and function of public sector labor unions, focusing in particular on teachers, reduced money for public education, and limited the amount of teachers' salaries that could go toward medical insurance. In essence, the measure forced a reduction in teachers' salaries while also stripping them of a voice in the matter.

Protests erupted at the capitol in Madison, and Democratic legislators left Wisconsin to prevent having a quorum to vote on the budget. For some three weeks in February and March, crowds estimated at up to 100,000 people occupied the capitol and capitol grounds, sometimes in falling snow. A drum circle formed in the capitol rotunda, and people packed the rotunda and the two balconies. The noise level was intense. Celebrities such as Michael Moore addressed rallies.

I was on the second balcony of the capitol on the day that Jesse Jackson appeared on the first balcony and addressed the throng. The response to him thundered. I scurried down to the ground level, and managed to grasp his hand as he made his way out of the building with his other hand pressing a cell phone to his ear.

Outside the capitol, crowds roamed the grounds, including mothers with small children in strollers, parents doing civics lessons with their children, groups of school children with signs supporting their teachers, and on and on. In support of the teachers' union, members of the Teamsters Union drove their big rigs in and parked on Capitol Square. I walked around the square with my daughter Lisa, a teacher in the Madison school system, shaking hands with teamsters and thanking them for their support. I grew up with a commitment to passive nonresistance and the belief that labor unions were wrong because strikes exerted force. As we thanked Teamsters for coming, I was quite aware of the juxtaposition with my early beliefs.

Eventually the capitol building itself was cleared of protestors and a perimeter set up outside, a few feet from the building. A favorite memory comes from the time I went to the protest with my friend Earl Zimmerman, who was interim pastor at Madison Mennonite Church, on the day that Governor Walker was scheduled to give the State of the State address. Earl and I worked our way up to the restraining rope at the top of the steps on the State Street entrance to the capitol. The chanting of slogans was intense, making it difficult to talk. A state trooper emerged from a door of the capitol and walked the ten feet to our location at the top of the steps. He told the gathered crowd, "Walker can hear you, and boy is he pissed." The already deafening noise reached yet another decibel louder.

In contrast to the storming of the Capitol in Washington, D.C. on 6 January 2021, despite the enormous crowds and the packed capitol building, the protests in Madison were overwhelmingly, intentionally nonviolent. A Fox News report described the "near riot" conditions in Madison, but their own report belied that claim when the fighting they showed was occurring amid palm trees, which do not grow in Madison's cli-

mate! Madison's reputation for humor went on full display
when protestors started appearing with fake palm trees. Virtually every member of Madison Mennonite Church participated
at least one day in the protests.

Involvement in these protests constituted a prime example
of the idea that it is possible to work with others on a common
concern without first settling underlying differences. For example, I attended a rally sponsored by Iraq Veterans Against the
War. These Iraq war veterans made clear that although they
were not pacifists, they opposed the war in Iraq. They supported
the protests, and believed that the money wasted on the war in
Iraq would more than fund the cuts in the budget proposed by
the Republican governor. I did not need to discuss pacifism and
violence with these men and women to participate in their rally
whose purpose I supported.

A major publication effort, begun not long after we moved to
Madison, was producing the second edition of *The Nonviolent
Atonement*. When the first edition appeared in 2001, nonviolent
atonement was a new idea and my book was the first major articulation of it. In it, I wrote responses to the efforts to defend
Anselmian atonement against charges such as "divine child
abuse." I dealt with seven, all but one of which were articles, in
eight pages, plus analyzing a longer statement for which I used
eight pages.

By the time of the second edition, writing about atonement
had become virtually a cottage industry. A number of collections
of essays had appeared. I responded to five additional major defenses of traditional, satisfaction atonement, most of them in
book-length treatments, as well as comparing my approach to
nine other articulations of nonviolent atonement. The second
edition was one hundred pages longer than the first.

Further, two publications made major contributions to the
second edition of *The Nonviolent Atonement*. One was David
Brondos's *Paul on the Cross*. Brondos, a Lutheran professor of
theology and Bible at the Theological Community of Mexico, a
consortium of seminaries in Mexico City, recognized my name
badge at a meeting of American Academy of Religion and asked
to chat. He suggested that I check out his book *Paul on the*

Cross, which he thought was compatible with what I was writing about atonement.

I was pleased to tell him that I was already reading material for the second edition, and I just happened to have his book on my desk, the first thing I would pick up when I got home. Brondos was right. He wrote that the entire corpus of Paul's writing supports nonviolent atonement, and that Paul should not be treated as the forerunner of Anselm's satisfaction atonement, as supporters of the traditional view have claimed. I used Brondos' book to make a major addition and improvement in my discussion of the apostle Paul.

The second book important for my second edition was *Saving Paradise* by Rita Nakishima Brock and Rebecca Parker. They wrote that in the early church, the cross was a symbol of resurrection and life. Paradise, as in Jesus' promise to the thief on the cross, was an earthly realm in which the saints waited with Jesus until the last judgment and transport to a faraway heaven. Iconography in a church depicted this arrangement—worshipers entered the church on the earthly level, higher on the walls were images of Jesus as the good shepherd with his sheep and then the image of God in heaven on the ceiling.

Emperor Charlemagne was crowned emperor by Pope Leo III on Christmas Day in the year 800. Images of Jesus' suffering and crucifixion appeared only after Saxon Christians experienced severe violence at the hands of the Carolingian Christian Empire. The first surviving crucifix with a dead Jesus, the Gero Cross, was produced about 960-970. The transition from cross as symbol of resurrection and life to focus on death reached its conclusion with Anselm, whose *Cur Deus Homo* does not even mention resurrection.

I described Jesus' confrontation of evil, his death, and then resurrection as a Christus Victor atonement image; that is an image in which evil powers killed Jesus but the reign of God was victorious over evil in the resurrection. This image is also visible in the book of Revelation, where one observes that historical antecedents of Revelation's images depict the early church as it confronts the empire, with the triumph of the reign of God in the resurrection.

These observations mean that Christus Victor as nonviolent atonement corresponds to the church that is distinct from the state church. This status of the church confronting empire disappeared as the church accepted empire and became a mass church or established church. Anselm's satisfaction atonement replaced the nonviolent Christus Victor as atonement image. As described by Brock and Parker, the transition from cross as symbol of life and resurrection to Anselm's focus on Jesus' death with no mention of resurrection fit my argument precisely. Brock and Parker's argument became a significant addition to the second edition of *The Nonviolent Atonement*, which appeared in 2011.

In the conclusion to *The Nonviolent Atonement* I wrote that throughout the book, the argument implied that the God of Jesus and of nonviolent atonement was a nonviolent God. It was a view that I had come to believe and understood as integral to the development of nonviolent atonement but without making an extended statement about God.

In spring 2006 I had given the C. Henry Smith peace lecture on the nonviolence of God, and the idea was integral to the discussion of nonviolent atonement. But after *The Nonviolent Atonement* was concluded, it became evident to me that I needed to make it explicit about the character of God. The result was *The Nonviolent God*, published in 2013. In this book, I pushed beyond several earlier Mennonite statements. John Howard Yoder had preserved a nonviolent approach to God and the Bible by arguing that divine commands in the Old Testament to massacre enemies were about obedience rather than about killing.

In his book *Yahweh is a Warrior*, Millard Lind took a step away from violent images of God. He argued that God's primary means of fighting were not with human armies and weapons but through nature. The paradigmatic example was the exodus, in which the Israelites escaped the pursuing, Egyptian army through the miracle that parted the Reed Sea for their passage.

To me, such arguments avoided obvious elements of the biblical story. I adopted a view argued by several scholars, namely that the Old Testament actually had a conversation about the character of God and divine violence. Alongside the accounts of commands to massacre enemies and of God's destruction of the wicked are also stories that depicted representatives of God's people as they avoided violence or dealt with enemies without violence, often with divine help.

Among many examples are the account in Judges 6 of Gideon's rout of the Midianites with a small band of men and a ruse, the story in 2 Kings 6 of Elisha's turning away an Aramean invasion by feeding the invading army, and the cultural resistance of the Hebrew captives in the book of Daniel. The question then became which of these images of God was the correct one. When one understands that Jesus is a direct continuation and descendant of the Israelites depicted in the Old Testament, it becomes clear that the nonviolent image of God is the one revealed in the narrative of the Jesus who rejected violence. This insight puts a premium on the conclusion that the New Testament narrative of Jesus is the basis for the discussion of Christology, following the example of the statements in the book of Acts that show how the apostles identified Jesus by telling his story in the months immediately after his death and resurrection (2:14-39; 3:13-26; 4:10-12; 5:30-32; 10: 36-43; 13:17-41).

After summarizing atonement, and discussion of God and Christology, *The Nonviolent God* dealt with nonviolence, racism, gender issues, economics, forgiveness, and the natural world. Ron Adams, pastor of Madison Mennonite Church, with whom I met frequently for lunch, served as reader and adviser as I worked on the manuscript.

Moving to Madison, Wisconsin, upon retirement provided multiple opportunities for ecumenical cooperation. Ron Adams took the initiative that made Mennonites members of the Wisconsin Council of Churches. Since membership is by judicatories, the actual member of the Wisconsin Council is Central District Conference. In fact, Central District Conference has only two congregations located in Wisconsin. Ron Adams attended the annual meeting of the Council as the official Mennonite delegate, and I served as the Mennonite representative to the Peace and Justice Commission, a position I held for seven years.

When *The Nonviolent God* appeared, the Commission adopted it for the year's theological reading, and some chapters were discussed at each quarterly meeting. When the Commission had a focus on anti-racism, I did a series of three video presentations—on Jesus and racism, on the way that traditional theology has accommodated racism, and on the biblical foundation for nonviolent activism—which were posted on the Wisconsin Council's website as supplementary material to the study guide on anti-racism. The two directors of the Council with whom I served supplied endorsements for the back cover of the two editions of *God Without Violence*.

Contacts through the Wisconsin Council of Churches resulted in a number of speaking opportunities in Madison. For Methodists, Moravians, Episcopalians, Lutherans, and United Church of Christ I spoke on various combinations of nonviolent atonement, nonviolent God, Black theology, and the biblical basis of nonviolent activism. Such experiences made very clear to me that since all Christians profess faith in Jesus, it is possible to articulate theology derived from Jesus for a general audience but that expresses the Anabaptist, peace church emphasis on Jesus' rejection of violence.

Although I was officially retired from Bluffton University, I did not retire from ongoing theological conversations. On my side of the conversation, my question was to figure out what theology looked like if one believed that God was revealed in the Jesus who rejected violence. This effort involved both critique of the received, presumed standard tradition, and articulation of alternatives. I focused on atonement imagery and Christology.

Along the way, the critique of the tradition produced resistance. Summarizing responses from Stanley Hauerwas, Ron Sider, and Darrin Snyder Belousek is instructive. All three advocate pacifism, but all three offered major rejections of my atonement imagery and approach to Christology. Hauerwas favors a high church ecclesiology with pacifism as a cultural norm. He fears that a believers church ecclesiology, which lacks a hierarchical teaching office à la Catholicism, a robust sacramentalism, and a Nicene Christology will be captured by liberal impulses and end up with nothing but peace as an ethical kernel. He simply laughs at the contradiction between a commitment to pacifism and the accommodation of violence in classic Christology and atonement images.

Conservative, sometimes in my assessment quasi-fundamentalist critic Ron Sider believes that I am not true to the Old Testament, that I reject biblical atonement, and that we do not know enough to know how to reconcile all biblical material on God's violence with Jesus' example of nonviolence. Starting with the satisfaction image, Sider considers all three classic atonement images—Christus Victor, satisfaction, and moral influence—as unquestioned givens into which biblical texts can be inserted. Thus he deemphasizes the contexts in which they originated and the fact that each rejected the previous one.

Darrin Snyder Belousek charges me with failure to adhere to the Nicene Creed. He engages in a great deal of scholastic argument to claim that in line with classic Nicene and trinitarian doctrine, God is fully revealed in the Jesus who rejected violence while also maintaining the biblical images of the God who employs violence. My short answer to all three is to recall JoAnne Terrell's statement, namely that "God never wrote any theology." With that in mind, I need not suspend my mind or ignore contradictions to retain images of a violent God alongside nonviolent Jesus who revealed God, as do Hauerwas and Sider, nor engage in significant manipulation of logic, ã la Snyder Belousek, to say that Nicea's equation of Jesus with the Father nonetheless allows divine violence.

In contrast, my versions of Christology and atonement, which are not captive to traditional images raised to the level of unquestioned, transcendent givens, lack the inconsistencies of these writers. I addressed these issues in more detail, with footnotes to writings of Hauerwas, Sider, and Belousek, in an article in the Winter 2006 issue of *Conrad Grebel Review*.

Others welcomed my efforts to develop theology from an Anabaptist perspective. In 2015 I served on the dissertation committees of two young scholars who recruited me specifically because of my approach to theology. Drew Hart wrote his dissertation on a conversation between Anabaptism and Black theology. Drew placed me on his committee since I was the only

Mennonite theologian who had dealt extensively with black and womanist theology. Justin Heinzekehr brought his interest in process theology and Anabaptism together by writing a dissertation that developed a process approach to Christology from an Anabaptist perspective. Justin invited me to participate on his committee since, as he said, I was one of the few Mennonites doing theology from an Anabaptist perspective.

I produced two items aimed specifically at non-specialist and lay audiences. Both involved collaboration with our daughter, Lisa Weaver, who lives in Madison. Lisa recruited me to be co-author with her on the manuscript that became *Living the Anabaptist Story*. She developed the idea after her son, Simon, had a school assignment to write about his family history. After Simon asked me for information on Anabaptist history, the idea occurred to Lisa that most Mennonite young people did not have a grandfather who could talk about Anabaptist history. She decided to fill that void with a book on Anabaptist history for young people, and she recruited me to help with the project. We had distinct roles, and the cooperation worked well. Based primarily but not exclusively on *Becoming Anabaptist*, I provided the content, while Lisa put it in language accessible to young people and generally managed the project through its several iterations until its publication in 2015.

Numerous people had asked for a shorter and less academic statement of nonviolent atonement and nonviolent God. I set out to write a book that presented these issues in a format suitable for discussion in Sunday school classes, lay study groups, and introductory college classes. My first try, an effort to summarize the earlier books, bogged down and ground to a frustrating halt. I turned to my teacher-daughter Lisa for guidance.

We sat in her small computer room, Lisa at her keyboard. Lisa said, "Just forget about summarizing what you have already done." That startled me. In full teacher mode, Lisa continued, "Now, tell me the ten most important points you want to make with this book." After a few moments of thought, I listed ten points. As I talked, Lisa typed into a computer file. Then she continued, "Give me three points under each of those ten points." That was a bit harder; for at least one, I had only two points, but

I gave three points for the others. Then came the conclusion. My teacher said, "You have your outline. Your assignment is to sit at your computer and write a complete draft from this outline, without looking at any of your books or notes." I had my assignment, and I did my homework. Only after I had the first draft did I look up Scripture texts or find specific references to cite. *God Without Violence* appeared in 2016.

This approach to writing *God Without Violence* produced a surprise. Once it was finished, I noticed that the book's outline differed from the earlier books, particularly *The Nonviolent God*. For this popular edition, I sketched my narrative approach to atonement and Christology and located the discussion of the history of atonement and of Christology in chapters at the end of the book, as illustrations of how theology changes over time and in different contexts. Previously I had integrated my own approach into the historical discussions. In the preface I wrote that others should tell me if this different outline was significant.

Soon after *God Without Violence* appeared in 2016, I realized the significance of the changed outline. I had recently written an article "From Narrative Comes Theology," which appeared in the Spring 2016 issue of *Conrad Grebel Review*. In this article, I sketched my understanding of how theology develops as an extension of or an application of the narrative of Jesus as given in the New Testament. Soon after the appearance of *God Without Violence*, I realized that the book was not only a theological synthesis but a full-length example of the approach described in the article. When I had the opportunity to produce a second and revised edition, I made that methodology explicit.

In October 2015, Bluffton University hosted a major conference on Mennonite education, sponsored by the C. Henry Smith Trust and Mennonite Historical Society. I was asked to edit a book of presentations from the conference. I participated in the conference and along with editing, I wrote two essays for the book. The C. Henry Smith Trust sponsored the conference, which made it appropriate that when the book appeared in 2017 as *Education with the Grain of the Universe*, it was volume 11 in the C. Henry Smith Series. The grain of the universe reflects the nonviolent character of the Creator God, who is revealed in the

story of the Jesus who rejected violence. I edited the book to re-
flect issues of nonviolence and social justice in education for
Mennonites. It seemed like a volume 2 after *Teaching Peace* that
Gerald Mast and I edited in 2003.

In April 2018 J. Kameron Carter, author of *Race: A Theological Account*, was in Madison for the Lyons Lecture. The lecture was an annual event, sponsored by First Methodist Church,
a downtown church just off the Capitol Square. Carter's book
traced the origin of racism in Western theology back to the separation of Jesus from his Jewishness by the early church fathers,
as is visible in the formulas from the councils of Nicea and Chalcedon that defined Jesus as deity and humanity. These formulas
enabled Europeans to define their whiteness as the epitome of
what it meant to be human, and to envision Jesus in their own
white image.

This orientation of white supremacy then served to justify
the slave trade and the efforts by Europeans to colonize people
of color around the world. It was material from Carter that I incorporated into the revised edition of *God Without Violence* and
used in the new book, *Nonviolent Word*. It seems to me that for
anyone who has read the critique by Black scholars such as
James Cone and J. Kameron Carter, it should no longer be possible to cite the conciliar formulas without serious qualification.
After his lecture, I shook hands with Carter and said that I had
made use of his book *Race* in recent writing. He returned the
compliment. He recognized my name and mentioned my book
on atonement. When I had him autograph my copy of *Race*, he
wrote: "I am so blessed by your scholarship." That was a very
satisfying comment coming near the end of my formal career.

FOUR

END GAME

28

Year 2020

The year 2020 became an unforgettable year for reasons both bad and good. The coronavirus, often called Covid-19, entered the United States in mid-January. By mid-March, it had spread to the point that much of the economy shut down, meetings and programs of all kinds ceased in-person activity. Madison Mennonite Church began meeting on Zoom. My wife and I went out in public infrequently and wore masks when we did venture out. It became clear that the federal government was doing little to combat the spread of the virus, and by the end of the year about 350,000 people had died from the virus.

In 2020, deaths of African-Americans at the hands of police awakened the nation to the racial disparity in policing. On March 13, Breonna Taylor, a 26-year-old medical technician, was shot and killed by police in Louisville, Kentucky, who broke into her apartment, which was not the one on their search warrant. On 25 May, in Minneapolis, Minnesota, George Floyd died when a white police officer knelt on his neck for 9 minutes and 29 seconds although Floyd said numerous times that "I can't breathe." These two deaths precipitated Black Lives Matter demonstrations in many cities across the United States. As many readers will attest, discussions of white privilege, and the existence of one system of justice for Black people and another for white people, entered the public consciousness more than anytime in recent memory.

On the personal side, work I had begun earlier came to fruition so that 2020 became the year of three books. One was the appearance of the second, expanded edition of *God Without Violence*. I added comments on methodology, making explicit that the book illustrated my understanding that Christian theology develops as extensions or applications of the narrative of Jesus. I also added a statement on restorative justice, expanded the discussion of racism and Black theology, and added a comment on the Doctrine of Discovery. Finally, I wrote a new chapter on nonviolent activism.

A second book was *Nonviolent Word: Anabaptism, the Bible, and the Grain of the Universe*, co-written with Gerald Mast. This book included chapters based on presentations that Gerald and I gave in three venues: a conference at Baylor University on the Bible and the Reformation; a Believers Church Conference on ecumenical and global perspectives at Goshen College; and a faculty colloquium at Bluffton University. Gerald was the first author of the chapters on the sixteenth century, and I was first author of chapters with a contemporary focus as well as one sixteenth-century chapter.

This book presented the grain of the universe as a contemporary equivalent to the Word of the Bible, which produces the nonviolent Word. With its two parts on the sixteenth-century Anabaptism and a contemporary restatement, we looked as this book as a volume two after our earlier *Defenseless Christianity*. Two of my chapters dealt with racism and dialogue with the Black church, and with nonviolent activism. These chapters, as well as the material on Black theology and nonviolent activism in *God Without Violence*, were written before the tragic deaths of Breonna Taylor and George Floyd and the many demonstrations that followed. However, it seemed providential that this content appeared amid these demonstrations and the heightened awareness of racism and white privilege.

The third book of 2020 was *Mennonites in Madison*, co-authored with Lisa Weaver. It recounts the history of Madison Mennonite Church that began with a graduate student fellowship organized in 1960 by Theron Schlabach. We began by interviewing members from each epoch of the church. Using these interviews, I wrote a first draft, which we showed to church members and solicited comments and additions. With these suggestions, I requested files from longtime member Leila Shenk, who has maintained extensive records of the congregation since its official founding in 1987. These materials added significantly to the next draft, which Lisa edited. With Madison Mennonite member and graphic artist Hannah Sandvold handling design, the result was an illustrated book of some 120 pages. The first copies arrived the last week of 2020.

What became the last item that I worked on along with writing this memoir actually began more than a decade earlier. In June 2009 with support of four Anabaptist and Mennonite scholarly societies, Bluffton University hosted a major conference on Pilgram Marpeck. The conference theme, "Anabaptist Convictions After Marpeck," indicated that it dealt with both sixteenth-century and modern applications of Marpeck.

Gerald Mast, the Bluffton organizer of the conference, persuaded me to submit a paper for the conference and supplied the idea to which I followed. I wrote as a counter to the several scholars who claim that Marpeck's theology was a flawed version of trinitarian orthodoxy, and who depicted him as a mediator between literalist and spiritualist Anabaptists, or between Anabaptists and Catholics. In my paper, I pointed out that Marpeck had few references to the Trinity. He had none in his early tract, *Exposé of the Babylonian Whore*, in which he castigated the Reformers who sought to defend the new faith with the sword, hardly the language of a moderate mediator. Rather than characterizing him as a trinitarian who followed the theology of the church he rejected, I argued that Marpeck's theological approach was better understood as that of an Anabaptist shaped by the narrative of Jesus who rejected the sword.

A series of papers from the Marpeck conference were selected for publication in a volume of the C. Henry Smith Series. Gerald Mast and Trevor Bechtel, professor of ethics at Bluffton, began the editing process. After a series of delays, I was invited to serve as lead editor, and to finish the project. The volume on Marpeck was the last that I dealt with as editor of the C. Henry Smith Series. It was also the second book on which I worked with Gerald Mast as a co-editor. Files for this book on Marpeck were sent to the publisher amid writing this memoir.

For some twenty-five years—ten as colleagues in Bluffton and fifteen as long distance colleagues after I retired from teaching—Gerald Mast and I have been collaborators and conversation partners. With our offices in Bluffton a stairwell apart, we had innumerable conversations in one office or another, pushing our differing perspectives or working on projects together. Since my move to Madison, frequent consultation has continued via email and Zoom. We attended many conferences together, both before and after my retirement, on Anabaptist history and contemporary issues on Anabaptist or Mennonite themes, as is displayed in at least five published collections of papers in which we each have a chapter. Further, we have co-authored four articles and two books, and co-edited two books.

An important dimension of our cooperation is that both of us are committed to the Jesus of the New Testament that rejected the sword, and that we see Anabaptism as a distinct tradition that circles back to that Jesus as the source for understanding how the contemporary church lives in and engages the world. Thus each of us sees Anabaptism as a stance on which to develop a comprehensive outlook that addresses all Christians.

However, we approach these commitments from different disciplinary perspectives. I have entered our discussions from a perspective focused on postmodern theology, while Gerald speaks as a scholar of rhetoric, with questions about sixteenth-century Anabaptism. These different approaches mean that rather than being competitors, our views are mutually enriching; we learn from each other. From Gerald, I have learned about the analysis of an argument and how to argue an effective case. Gerald has also kept me from drifting completely away from my graduate work in sixteenth-century Anabaptism.

Through my influence, Gerald has learned about the particular or contextual character of the standard approach to theology, and the contributions of black, feminist, and womanist theologies. These two disciplinary approaches complement each other.

Nonetheless, on occasion we have approached a controversial issue with different impulses. Gerald's temperament and approach are to enter a discussion and make an argument in a way that brings as many people along as possible. In contrast, for me, the mentality that long ago pursued the correct answer to math problems has pushed me to make the strongest theological argument possible, even if the answer is controversial. For their amusement, analysts can peruse our co-written books for traces of this difference. Meanwhile, in only one instance did we start and then abandon a joint book project, the one that I pursued solo as *The Nonviolent God*.

The 29 June 2020 issue of *Mennonite World Review* carried a half-page feature on the collaboration that Gerald Mast and I have carried on for some twenty-five years. It is fitting that the Marpeck book, the last book project outlined in this memoir, is a collaborative effort with Gerald as well as with Trevor Bechtel. Gerald enticed me to contribute a paper to the conference from which the chapters of the book have come and then to become the lead editor.

Since the book and my contributions deal with sixteenth-century Anabaptism, it brings together the beginning and the end of my career, in conversation with my frequent collaborator. Sixty years ago, at Hesston College, my Uncle Gideon Yoder described the Elkhart Team and the Goshen Team. If he were alive today, this book on Marpeck would be one of the many items that might lead him to describe the Bluffton Team of J. Denny Weaver and Gerald J. Mast.

Conclusion

Although I did not recognize it at the time, the formal beginning of my career as a theologian came in 1974, when I asked if there was an Anabaptist or a Mennonite way to talk about issues such as Christology, atonement, and Trinity, and received no answer. I have spent the forty-plus years since then pursuing an answer to that question. Over time, the question evolved. I asked whether there was a specifically believers church way to express Christology.

Eventually, I focused the question in terms of what theology looked liked that was specific to Jesus and how Jesus' nonviolence was reflected in theology. Since all Christians profess Jesus as savior, these latter versions of the questions had an ecumenical dimension, but I hoped that even if I did not refer to them by name, Anabaptists and Mennonites as peace churches would recognize that the approach certainly included them.

When I first began asking about a theology for Mennonites, Anabaptism was popular, and there were jokes about an Anabaptist perspective on everything, even basket weaving. Thus when I began asking about an Anabaptist or Mennonite perspective on theology, I thought that my efforts would be welcomed. To my surprise, as the previous pages recount, there was significant resistance from Mennonites, along with the positive responses. At times, the positive responses from other Christians outnumbered those from Mennonites.

Under that broad agenda of theology addressed to all Christians, I wanted to show that theology makes a difference; it has the power to shape how people understand the world. For example, time-honored, traditional creedal language from the third and fourth centuries did not challenge the church's accommodation of the sword, and has allowed the development of white supremacy and the racism that undergirded slavery and the slave trade, the colonial empires, and the racism that still plagues many countries.

Anselmian, satisfaction atonement has modeled submission to unjust suffering, which is particularly harmful for women in situations of abuse, for enslaved people, and for people experiencing the injustice today of political, colonial, and economic domination. In contrast, my constructive effort was to develop theology that shaped ways to live that reflected the nonviolence of Jesus while confronting the injustice in the world.

As I pursued this agenda, some critics said that I pursued arguments competitively, even stubbornly. I actually agree. Much earlier in my life, I studied mathematics. The mentality that long ago relished mathematics also functioned for me in theology. Problems in mathematics had answers, and one persevered until that answer was found. Theology is a human construct with questions that also have answers. My persistence in theology through the years focused on figuring out what theology looked like for some important questions if one believed that God is revealed in the Jesus who rejected violence.

When there were objections to my theology, I sought to respond. I was not content to let a critique stand. If what I wrote had a problem, I wanted to fix it, just as I worked to find the error in a complicated math problem. My intent was to answer every challenge, answer every question. If that is called competitive, so be it. In a sense, I never stopped functioning as a mathematician.

With my theological efforts, my intent was to develop alternatives to theologies that contribute to injustice. I suggested that we identify Jesus by the narrative of his life, which makes his rejection of violence and the sword an integral dimension of theology. I developed an understanding of atonement that featured an activist Jesus. This image of Jesus supported women who suffered abuse rather than modeling their submission to it.

This atonement image equally supported resistance to slavery and racism in all forms rather than modeling submission to enslavers and unjust suffering. In this writing, my use of black theology, womanist theology, and feminist theology, more specific use made than by any other Mennonite male theologian, were major impulses in making these justice issues visible in my theology.

For those who were reluctant to worship a God of great violence, I provided an understanding of a nonviolent God, a God of love and mercy, who restored life rather than taking it. For those who struggled with a violent Bible, I offered a logical, alternative way to read the whole Bible and take it seriously. For those concerned for social justice on any number of fronts, I offered a wide-ranging view of nonviolent activism.

Along with these important elements of my theological production are some additional, original contributions. One concerned my description of the two continua, one describing nonviolent means and the other depicting increasingly violent means. I argued that nonviolent activism occupied its own continuum, in contrast to the common assumption that it was a mid-point on one continuum that measured increasing levels of violence from nonresistance on one end to nuclear war on the other. It was a seemingly obvious point that needed spelling out.

Another original contribution was my rejection of two-kingdom theology and replacing it with the reign of God and the non-reign-of-God. This latter encompasses all structures and institutions that are not aligned with the reign of God. This suggestion describes two entities even as it avoids validating as God-ordained the violence-based ordering function of the non-reign-of-God.

In the perspective of recent history, these are all important contributions of my writing. If my writing is remembered, I hope at least that my work with atonement remains visible and relevant. I can count on at least a few more years. Alistar McGrath included an excerpt on violence in traditional atonement images from one of my articles in the fourth and fifth editions of his *The Christian Theology Reader*. In a section on "Salvation in Christ," the excerpt appears in the heady company of a list of 38 names that begins with Irenaeus and includes Athanasius, Augustine, Anselm, and John Calvin, as well as several contemporary names. I also have in mind the vignette in the Prologue of this memoir. Over the years, the atonement windmill that I was charging has become smaller. For example, in the 18 October 2011 issue of *Christian Century*, *The Nonviolent Atonement* is listed as one of the five currently essential books on atonement. The comment of the reviewer of the second edition of *The Nonviolent Atonement* actually addressed my audacious goal when he wrote that if Anselmian atonement would no longer convince readers today, "We may have J. Denny Weaver's book to thank for that." May it be so.

STORING THE PIECES

Ode to a Giraffe
By J. Denny Weaver

The wee giraffe, its neck sticking out,
arrived as a surprise sent by my brother,
a gift from someone he worked with,

who grooved on the story Gary told
about my challenge to Anselm,
whose atonement image still reigns

supreme after nearly a thousand years.
He dared to stick his neck out, she said,
he deserves a giraffe. This diminutive

friend now resides in the menagerie
under our window. Whenever it catches
my eye with its neck stretched out,

I remember my brother no longer living,
and the audacity of challenging
the sainted Archbishop, and the thrill

of writing theology surges once again.

Afterword

For important games in chess tournaments, each move is recorded. Games are then published with analysis of both mistakes and brilliant moves provided by commentators. This book functions like the commentary on a chess game—it records commentary on theological moves, both questionable and insightful, throughout my career that resulted in development of a distinct theological program.

Chess games end in draws or wins. The narrative described the development of my theology to its final result. In terms of the chess metaphor, I have attempted to respond to all opposing moves, and I like my results. It remains for history to provide the ultimate judgment on whether it is actually a winning theology. As is true for chess, I continue to believe that some moves in theology prove problematic and should be abandoned or rejected. The narrative sketches my alternatives to problematic views.

But the narrative also displays that developing theology is far more than a game. Theology deals with real issues, and it has shaped how people have interacted with the world, acquiescing to violence, abetting colonialism, and encouraging submission to injustice, but also modeling actions that confront such injustice.

Different from chess, the narrative has displayed that developing theology involves participation in a wider conversation. When the first edition of *The Nonviolent Atonement* appeared in 2001, it was considered a ground-breaking book. In it, I dealt with seven authors whose articles defended satisfaction atonement against the charge that it was harmful for women or a purveyor of violence, and in conversation with writers of black, feminist, and womanist theology, the book provided an extended development of nonviolent atonement.

By the time of the second edition of 2011, writing on atonement had become a virtual cottage industry. For the second edition of 2011, in additional to the initial defenses, I responded to five major, mostly book-length defenses of satisfaction atonement while also engaging conversation with nine additional versions of nonviolent atonement or alternatives to the satisfaction image.

The second edition also added additional supportive material from other scholars. While I developed a distinct approach to atonement, it was a collaborative effort, done in conversation with biblical scholars, and writers of black, womanist, and feminist theology. The mutual stimulation of theology is also visible in the appearance of the nine other versions of nonviolent atonement, all working to pose an alternative to the received, standard tradition. Theology does not all develop in the same direction, and my effort does reject some efforts. But my program for nonviolent atonement and the additional suggestions for Christology and an array of other issues proceeds in company of others, all engaged in a wide-ranging conversation with many allies.

May this witness live and prosper.

Bibliography

Anselm of Canterbury. "Why God Became Man." In *The Major Works*, ed. & intro. by Brian Davies and G. R. Evans, 260–356. Oxford, UK: Oxford University Press, 1998.

Aulén, Gustaf. *Christus Victor: A Historical Study of the Three Main Types of the Idea of Atonement*. Trans. A. G. Herbert. New York: Macmillan Publishing, 1969.

Baker-Fletcher, Garth Kasimu. *Xodus: An African-American Male Journey*. Minneapolis: Fortress Press, 1996.

Baker-Fletcher, Karen, and Garth KASIMU Baker-Fletcher. *My Sister, My Brother: Womanist and XODUS God-Talk*. Bishop Henry McNeal Turner/Sojourner Truth Series in Black Religion, vol. 12. Maryknoll, New York: Orbis Books, 1997.

Bender, Harold S. *The Anabaptist Vision*. Scottdale, Pa.: Herald Press, 1944.

———. *Conrad Grebel c.1498–1526: The Founder of the Swiss Brethren Sometimes Called Anabaptists*.second printing. 1950. Studies in Anabaptist and Mennonite History, no. 6. Scottdale, Pa.: Herald Press, 1971.

Biesecker-Mast, Gerald. *Separation and the Sword in Anabaptist Persuasion: Radical Confessional Rhetoric from Schleitheim to Dordrecht*. The C. Henry Smith Series, vol. 6. Telford, Pa.: Cascadia Publishing House, 2006.

Biesecker-Mast, Susan, and Gerald Biesecker-Mast, eds. *Anabaptists and Postmodernity*. With a foreword by J. Denny Weaver. The C. Henry Smith Series, vol. 1. Telford, Pa.: Pandora Press U.S.; copublished with Herald Press, 2000.

Boyarin, Daniel. *Border Lines: The Partition of Judaeo-Christianity*. Philadelphia: University of Pennsylvania Press, 2004.

Brock, Rita Nakashima, and Rebecca Ann Parker. *Saving Paradise: How Christianity Traded Love of This World for Crucifixion and Empire*. Boston: Beacon Press, 2008.

Brondos, David A. *Paul on the Cross: Reconstructing the Apostle's Story of Redemption*. Minneapolis: Fortress Press, 2006.

Brown, Joanne Carlson, and Carole R. Bohn, eds. *Christianity, Patriarchy, and Abuse: A Feminist Critique*. New York: Pilgrim Press, 1989.

Burkholder, J. Lawrence. *The Problem of Social Responsibility from the Perspective of the Mennonite Church*. Elkhart, Ind.: Institute of Mennonite Studies, 1989.

Calvin, John. *Calvin: Institutes of the Christian Religion I*. Ed. John T. Nc-Neill. Trans & indexed Ford Lewis Battles. The Library of Christian Classics, Vol. 20. Philadelphia: The Westminster Press, 1960.

———. *Calvin: Institutes of the Christian Religion II*. Ed. John T. McNeill. Trans & indexed Ford Lewis Battles. The Library of Christian Classics, Vol. 21. Philadelphia: The Westminster Press, 1960.

Carter, J. Kameron. *Race: A Theological Account*. New York: Oxford University Press, 2008.

Cone, James H. *Black Theology and Black Power*. New York: Seabury, 1969.

———. *God of the Oppressed*. San Francisco: HarperSanFrancisco, 1975.

———. *God of the Oppressed*. Rev. ed. Maryknoll, NY: Orbis, 1997.

de Gaulle, Charles. *Mémoires de Guerre—Tome 1 l'Appel 1940–1942*. Paris, France: Pocket, 2010.

———. *Mémoires de Guerre—Tome 2 l'Unité 1942–1944*. Paris, France: Pocket, 2010.

———. *Mémoires de Guerre—Tome 3 le Salut 1944–1946*. Paris, France: Pocket, 2010.

Dickinson, Colby. "The Nonviolent Atonement." Review of *The Nonviolent Atonement*. J. Denny Weaver. *Louvain Studies* 36, no. vol. 1 (2012): 103–04.

Dyer, Gwynne. *War: The Lethal Custom*. Rev. ed. New York: Carrol & Graf Publishers, 2004.

Enns, Fernando, Scott Holland, and Ann K. Riggs, eds. *Seeking Cultures of Peace: A Peace Church Conversation*. Telford, Pennsylvania: Cascadia Publishing House; copublisher, Herald Press, 2004.

Finger, Thomas N. *A Contemporary Anabaptist Theology: Biblical, Historical, Constructive*. Downers Grove, Ill.: InterVarsity Press, 2004.

"Friendship, Debate Link Bluffton Pair." *Mennonite World Review*, 29 June 2020, 20.

Heim, S. Mark, ed. *Faith to Creed: Ecumenical Perspectives on the Affirmation of the Apostolic Faith in the Fourth Century*. Grand Rapids, Michigan: William B. Eerdmans Publishing Company, 1991.

Hershberger, Guy Franklin. *The Way of the cross in Human Relations*. Scottdale, Pa.: Herald Press, 1958.

Hochschild, Adam. *King Leopold's Ghost: A Story of Greed, Terror, and Heroism in Colonial Africa*. Boston: Houghton Mifflin Company, 1998.

Kraus, C. Norman. *Jesus Christ Our Lord: Christology from a Disciple's Perspective*. Rev. ed. Scottdale, Pa.: Herald Press, 1990.

Lesher, Emerson L. *The Muppie Manual: The Mennonite Urban Professional's Handbook for Humility and Success or (How to Be the Gentle in the City)*. Intercourse, Pa.: Good Books, 1985.

Lind, Millard C. *Yahweh is a Warrior: The Theology of Warfare in Ancient Israel*. Scottdale, Pennsylvania: Herald Press, 1980.

Loewen, James W. *Lies My Teacher Told Me: Everything Your American History Textbook Got Wrong*. New York: Simon & Schuster, 1995.

Loyola, Ignacio de. *The Spiritual Exercises of St. Ignatius*. Trans. Anthony Mottola. Garden City, N. Y.: Image Books, 1964.

Luther, Martin. "Against the Robbing and Murdering Hordes of Peasants." In *Selected Writings of Martin Luther: 1523–1526*. Ed Theodore G. Tappert, 346–55. Philadelphia: Fortress Press, 1967.

———. "The Babylonian Captivity of the Church." In *Selected Writings of Martin Luther: 1517–1520*. Ed. Theodore G. Tappert, 355–478. Philadelphia: Fortress Press, 1967.

———. "The Freedom of a Christian." In *Selected Writings of Martin Luther: 1520–23*. Ed. Theodore G. Tappert, 3–53. Philadelphia.: Fortress Press, 1967.

———. "Ninety-Five Theses." In *Selected Writings of Martin Luther: 1517–1520*. Ed.Theodore G. Tappert, 43–59. Philadelphia: Fortress Press, 1967.

———. "To the Christian Nobility of the German Nation Concerning the Reform of the Christian Estate." In *Selected Writings of Martin Luther: 1517–1520*. Ed. Theodore G. Tappert, 251–353. Philadelphia: Fortress Press, 1967.

Mast, Gerald J., and J. Denny Weaver. *Defenseless Christianity: Anabaptism for a Nonviolent Church.* With a foreword by Greg Boyd. Telford, Pa.: Cascadia Publishing House; copublished with Herald Press, 2009.

McGrath, Alister E., ed. *The Christian Theology Reader,* fifth edition. Chichester, West Sussex, UK: Wiley-Blackwell, 2016.

McWilliams, David B. "The Nonviolent Atonement." Review of *The Nonviolent Atonement.* J. Denny Weaver. *Westminster Theological Review* 64, no. vol. 1 (2002): 117–20.

Sanders, John, ed. *Atonement and Violence: A Theological Conversation.* Nashville: Abingdon Press, 2006.

Sawatsky, Rodney J., and Scott Holland, eds. *The Limits of Perfection: A Conversation with J. Lawrence Burkholder.* second ed. Waterloo, Ont. and Kitchener, Ont.: Institute of Anabaptist and Mennonite Studies, Conrad Grebel College; and Pandora Press, 1993.

Stayer, James M., Werner O. Packull, and Klaus Deppermann. "From Monogenesis to Polygenesis: The Historical Discussion of Anabaptist Origins." *Mennonite Quarterly Review* 49, no. 2 (April 1975): 83–122.

Swartley, Willard, ed. *Explorations of Systematic Theology from Mennonite Perspectives.* Occasional Papers, No. 7. Elkhart, Indiana: Institute of Mennonite Studies, 1984.

van Braght, Thieleman J. *The Bloody Theater or Martyrs Mirror of the Defenseless Christians Who Baptized Only Upon Confession of Faith, and Who Suffered and Died for the Testimony of Jesus, Their Savior, from the Time of Christ to the Year A.D. 1660.* Trans. Joseph F. Sohm. Scottdale, Pa.: Mennonite Publishing House, 1950.

Waltner, Erland, ed. *Jesus Christ and the Mission of the Church: Contemporary Anabaptist Perspectives.* By George R. III Brunk, John E. Toews, Harry Huebner, and J. Denny Weaver, respondant Daniel D. Garcia, Mary H. Schertz, and Thomas Finger. Newton, Kansas: Faith and Life Press, 1990.

Weaver, Alain Epp, and Gerald J. Mast, eds. *The Work of Jesus Christ in Anabaptist Perspective: Essays in Honor of J. Denny Weaver.* With a foreword by Myron S. Augsburger. Telford, Pa.: Cascadia Publishing House; Scottdale, Pa.: Herald Press, 2008.

Weaver, J. Denny, ed. *Education with the Grain of the Universe: A Peaceable Vision for the Future of Mennonite Schools, Colleges, and Universities.* With a foreword by Susan Schultz Huxman. The C.

Henry Smith Series. Telford, Pa.: Cascadia Publishing House, 2017.

Weaver, J. Denny. "America Shouldn't Mirror ISIS Violence." *Wisconsin State Journal*, 6 April 2016, A9.

———. *Anabaptist Theology in Face of Postmodernity: A Proposal for the Third Millennium*. With a foreword by Glen Stassen. The C. Henry Smith Series, vol. 2. Telford, Pa.: Pandora Press U.S., copublished with Herald Press, 2000.

———. "Atonement for the NonConstantinian Church." *Modern Theology* 6, no. 4 (July 1990): 307–23.

———. *Becoming Anabaptist: The Origin and Significance of Sixteenth-Century Anabaptism*. Scottdale, Pa.: Herald Press, 1987.

———. *Becoming Anabaptist: The Origin and Significance of Sixteenth-Century Anabaptism*.second ed. With a foreword by William H. Willimon. Scottdale, Pa.: Herald Press, 2005.

———. "Christus Victor, Ecclesiology, and Christology." *Mennonite Quarterly Review* 68, no. 3 (July 1994): 277–90.

———. *"Confession of Faith in a Mennonite Perspective* in Missional Perspective." *Anabaptist Witness* 7, no. 1 (May 2020): 41–60.

———. "From Narrative Comes Theology." *The Conrad Grebel Review* 34, no. 2 (Spring 2016): 117–30.

———. *Gewaltfreie Erlösung: Kreuzestheologie im Ringen mit der Satifakionstheorie*, trans. Jörg Bráker, with a Foreword by Fernando Enns. Berlin: Lit Verlag: 2016.

———. *God Without Violence: A Theology of the God Revealed in Jesus*. Second, expanded ed. Eugene, Ore.: Cascade Books, 2020.

———. *God Without Violence: Following a Nonviolent God in a Violent World*. Eugene, Ore.: Cascade Books, 2016.

———, "Pacifism." In The Oxford Encyclopedia of the Reformation, I–IV, ed. Hans J. Hillerbrand. New York: Oxford University, 1996.

———. "Hubmaier Versus Hut on the Work of Christ: The Fifth Nicolsburg Article." *Archiv Für Reformationsgeschichte* 82 (1991): 171–92.

———. "In der 'Geschichte Jesu' Leben." *Mennonitische Geschichtsblätter* 63 (2006): 51–72.

———. "A Jesus-Centered Peace Theology, or, Why and How Theology and Ethics Are Two Sides of One Profession of Faith." *The Conrad Grebel Review* 34, no. 1 (Winter 2016): 5–27.

———. *Keeping Salvation Ethical: Mennonite and Amish Atonement Theology in the Late Nineteenth Century.* Foreword C. Norman Kraus. Studies in Anabaptist and Mennonite History. Scottdale, Pa.: Herald Press, 1997.

———. "Living in the Reign of God in the 'Real World': Getting Beyond Two-Kingdom Theology." In *Exiles in the Empire: Believers church Perspectives on Politics,* vol. 5. Ed. Nathan E. Yoder and Carol A. Scheppard. Studies in the Believers Church Tradition, 173–93. Kitchener, Ont.: Pandora Press, 2006.

———. *The Nonviolent Atonement.* Grand Rapids: Wm. B. Eerdmans Publishing Co., 2001.

———. *The Nonviolent Atonement.*second ed., greatly rev. and expanded. Grand Rapids: Wm. B. Eerdmans Publishing Co., 2011.

———. *The Nonviolent God.* Grand Rapids, Mich.: William B. Eerdmans Publishing Co., 2013.

———. "Perspectives on a Mennonite Theology." In *Explorations of Systematic Theology from Mennonite Perspectives.* Ed. Willard Swartley. Occasional Papers, 17–36. Elkhart, Ind.: Institute of Mennonite Studies, 1984.

———. "Perspectives on a Mennonite Theology." *The Conrad Grebel Review* 2, no. 3 (Fall 1984): 189–210.

———. "The Quickening of Soteriology: Atonement from Christian Burkholder to Daniel Kauffman." *Mennonite Quarterly Review* 61, no. 1 (January 1987): 5–45.

———. "Some Theological Implications of Christus Victor." *Mennonite Quarterly Review* 68, no. 4 (October 1994): 483–99.

———. "Think Outside the Box in North Korea." *Wisconsin State Journal,* 14 August 2017, A9.

———. "The Work of Christ: On the Difficulty of Identifying an Anabaptist Perspective." *Mennonite Quarterly Review* 59, no. 2 (April 1985): 107–29.

Weaver, J. Denny, and Gerald Biesecker-Mast, eds. *Teaching Peace: Nonviolence and the Liberal Arts.* Lanham, Md.: Rowman & Littlefield Publishers, Inc., 2003.

Weaver, J. Denny, ed., Earl Zimmerman, Zachary J. Walton, Gerald J. Mast, Ted Grimsrud, and Glen Harold Stassen. *John Howard Yoder: Radical Theologian.* With a foreword by Marva J. Dawn, with an afterword by Lisa Schirch. Eugene, Ore.: Cascade Books, 2014.

Weaver, J. Denny, and Gerald J. Mast. *Nonviolent Word: Anabaptism, the Bible, and the Graini of the Universe*. Eugene, Ore.: Pickwick Publications, 2020.

Weaver, J. Denny, and Lisa Weaver. *Mennonites in Madison: A History of Faith, Fellowship, & the Formation of a Congregation*. Madison, Wis.: MennoWorks, 2020.

Williams, Delores S. *Sisters in the Wilderness: The Challenge of Womanist God-Talk*. Maryknoll, New York: Orbis Books, 1993.

Williams, George Huntston, and Angel M. Mergal, eds. *Spiritual and Anabaptist Writers: Documents Illustrative of the Radical Reformation*. The Library of Christian Classics, vol. 25. Philadelphia: The Westminster Press, 1957.

Yoder, John Howard. *The Jewish-Christian Schism Revisited*. Ed. Michael G. Cartwright and Peter Ochs. Grand Rapids, Mich.: William B. Eerdmans Publishing Company, 2003.

———. *The Politics of Jesus: Vicit Agnus Noster*. 2nd ed. Grand Rapids, Mich.: William B. Eerdmans, 1994.

———. *Preface to Theology: Christology and Theological Method*. Elkhart, Ind.: Goshen Biblical Seminary; distributed by Co-Op Bookstore, 1981.

———. *Preface to Theology: Christology and Theological Method*. With an introduction by Stanley Hauerwas and Alex Sider. Grand Rapids, Mich.: Brazos Press, 2002.

Index of Names

J
Jackson, Jesse, 209
Jenkins, Philip, 189-90
Johns, Loren, 158

K
Kampen, John, 153-55, 162, 171-73
Karlstadt, Andreas, 205
Kennedy, Arthur, 182-83
Kennedy, John F., 52
King, Martin Luther, jr., 30, 133
King, Michael, 206
Klaassen Walter, 183
Krall, Ruth, 130-31
Kraus, C. Norman, 42-45, 56, 82, 85. 89, 112
Kreider, Robert, 136
Kushel, Ted, 95

L
Lehman, James O., 103
Lesher, Emerson, 76
Lewis, John, 173
Lind, Millard, 47-49, 71, 75, 80, 115, 212
Lind, Suzanne, 180
Lindsey, Hal, 186
Loewen, James, 168
Luther, Martin, 77-79, 81, 165, 182, 205

M
Marpeck, Pilgram, 157, 223, 225
Mast, Gerald J., 135-36, 154-55, 157-59, 161-64, 197, 201, 203, 205-06, 218, 222-25
McWilliams, David, 178
Menno Simons, 157, 204-05
Miller, Lynn, 185
Miller, Marlin 111-12
Montel, Angela, 164
Moore, Michael, 208
Moser, Johannes, 102-04
Moser, John, 104
Müntzer, Thiomas, 101

N
Nation, Mark Thiessen, 196
Neufeld, Elmer, 86, 89, 94-97, 102, 114, 122, 137-43
Nixon, Richard M., 52-53, 73

O
Oyer, John, 44-45

P
Packull, Werner, 100
Page, Alan, 168
Parker, Rebecca, 149-50, 177-78, 211-212
Parks, Rosa, 30
Pfeifer, Bob, 162
Preheim, Vern, 95, 97

R
Reimer, A. James, 94,112,134-36, 155-56, 181
Riggs, Ann, 180-82, 184
Robertson, Pat, 185

S
Sanders, John, 156, 178
Sandvold, Hannah, 223
Sattler, Michael, 100
Schirch, Lisa, 200-01
Schlabach, Theron, 99, 222
Shenk, Leila, 223
Shenk, Stanley, 86
Sider, Ron, 113-14, 116-17, 122, 142, 182, 214-15
Simons, Menno. *See* Menno Simons
Slotter, Arden, 136
Snyder, C. Arnold, 156
Snyder, Lee, 153-55, 170-72, 174
Sommer, Betty, 134, 149
Sprunger, Benjamin, 138
Stassen, Glen, 162-63, 183
Stauffer, Jacob, 102
Stayer, James, 100
Stoltzfus, Gene, 44, 106-07

Swartley, Willard, 94

T
Talavinia, Phill, 207-08
Terrell, JoAnne Marie, 169, 215
Tertullian, 182
Thistlethwaite, Susan Brooks, 167

V
Van Dyk, Leanne, 175-76
VandeEnde, Ted, 92-98, 112, 141, 182

W
Walker, Scott, 208-09
Waltner, Erland, 112-12, 115-17
Weaver, Alain Epp, 159, 161, 205
Weaver, Lisa, 209, 216, 222-23
Weaver, Michelle, 121
Weaver, Simon, 216
Weaver, Sonia, 159, 161
Wenger, John C., 79-80, 71-72
Wenger/Weaver, Mary Lois, 40, 50-51, 61, 64, 68, 76, 82, 87, 121, 190, 203-05
West, Cornel, 179
Westmoreland-White, Michael, 162-63
Williams, Delores, 151, 175
Wink, Walter, 175

Y
Yoder, Gideon G., 38, 39, 235
Yoder, J. Otis, 174
Yoder, John Howard, 85, 87-90, 113, 136, 155-56, 168, 196-202, 212
Yoder, Perry, 44

Z
Zimmerman, Earl, 196-97, 201, 209

The Author

J. Denny Weaver is Professor Emeritus of Religion, Bluffton (Ohio) University. He grew up in the Argentine district of Kansas City, Kansas, where the family attended Argentine Mennonite Church. He has a BA from Goshen College with a major in mathematics, an MDiv from what is now Anabaptist Mennonite Biblical Seminary, and a PhD from Duke University. His graduate school focus was the Protestant Reformation, with a major in Anabaptist theology.

He interrupted his seminary studies for a term of alternative service with Mennonite Central Committee, 1965-68. He and his wife Mary spent a year in French study in Belgium and France and then two years in Algeria where Weaver was teacher of English in an Algerian lycée. Following Algeria, they spent a year in Germany; there Weaver studied at Kirrchliche Hochschule Bethel at Bethel bei Bielefield.

Following graduation from Duke, Weaver spent a year as a sabbatical replacement at Goshen College and then moved to Bluffton, Ohio, where he served for thirty-one years as a member of the Religion Department of Bluffton University. He taught courses in church history, theology, and ethics.

He spent 1990-91 in Winnipeg, Manitoba, as Visiting Professor of Theology at what was then Canadian Mennonite Bible College. Weaver was the first editor of the C. Henry Smith Series, sponsored by Bluffton University, a role he held until 2020, producing thirteen volumes as senior CHS editor assessing and shaping Anabaptist-Mennonite scholarly works.

Weaver has written or edited many articles and books, ranging across Anabaptist theology, historical Mennonite theology, and contemporary systematic theology. His theological writing asked how the doctrines of atonement, Christology, and the character of God, may have contributed positively or negatively to issues of violence, racism, and the roles of women.

In the early 1990s, Weaver went to Haiti three times with delegations of Christian Peacemaker Teams, a nonviolent conflict reduction group. He has given invited lectures on atonement theology in the United Kingdom, in German in Germany, and in French in the Congo.

On retirement, Weaver and his wife Mary moved to Madison Wisconsin, where he has continued speaking and writing. He served for seven years as a member of the Peace and Justice Commission of the Wisconsin Council of Churches.

He and his wife now attend Madison Mennonite Church. They enjoy spending time with their three adult daughters and six grandchildren.

Printed in the USA
CPSIA information can be obtained
at www.ICGtesting.com
JSHW020924071223
53327JS00013B/117